THE PURSUIT OF FORGIVENESS 2.0

Unlocking Pragmatic Forgiveness

THE PURSUIT OF FORGIVENESS 2.0
Unlocking Pragmatic Forgiveness

ISBN: 978-1-7327804-7-7
The Pursuit of Forgiveness
Copyright © 2015
Copyright © 2019
by Melissa Reese, The Pursuit Guru

Printed in the United States.

The "Inside-Flap Teaser" . . .

Why is it so hard to let go, move on, and be happy? How and where do you even start to be able to forgive?

Pragmatic forgiveness is as essential, basic, dynamic, and profound as eating. There is the concept of forgiveness, and then there is the actual application of *it*. This book offers the opportunity to truly understand forgiveness and actually implement it for oneself. It provides a nonreligious approach to utilizing forgiveness—intended to capture all human beings, no matter what "compartment" they've placed themselves in: religious, spiritual, agnostic, atheist, nothing, or "I don't know." This book encourages people to get past what they "think" they know as true and into what they "feel" they know is true, for themselves—regardless of any other expectations or limitations.

Here is your guide to understanding forgiveness, knowing how and when to implement it, and creating your life.

This book has downloadable audio to help with the process. www.thepursuitofforgiveness.com

The *Pursuit of Forgiveness* is a fast-track path on how to live a life of fulfillment. [In this] well-written and well-documented look at life from the perspective of true forgiveness, one realizes that truly being alive starts with forgiveness. Intellectual, emotional, and spiritual examples and *lessons* fill the pages with the why and how-to of forgiveness.

Melissa clearly shows us the results of not forgiving ("disassociating") and fully forgiving ("disconnecting"). The *Pursuit of Forgiveness* is a must-read guidebook of forgiveness and a call to action to forgive those parts of your life that need forgiveness, not sometime but now!

And if you think reading Melissa's book is compelling, wait until you meet her—she is an inspired, stand-for-change, and well-being person! I will be sharing this incredible gem with family, friends, and clients alike.

—Thom Wells, Thomas Wells Companies

Contents

Forgiveness is the act of freeing your heart from the clasp you have allowed others to restrict you with.

—*Kurt Hickenlooper*

Acknowledgments

I have been given the gift of forgiveness, and I choose to accept it. I continue to choose to accept it and employ it.

Thank you to . . .
My husband, family, friends, teachers, mentors, perfect strangers, et al.

Jan, my Jan, I am so very grateful for all your tireless hours of reading and feedback over the years. Linda, thank you for your fantastic feedback and insight. Mom, thank you for your insight. Nick, thank you for your willingness to grow, evolve, love, and support yourself and me. Kurt, rest in peace and LOVE—thank you for your heartfelt and generous contributions.

I am forever a student and in gratitude, even when it's f*cking *hard*.

How can forgiveness change your life? How can it help improve your physical, mental, and emotional health? Here is your guide to what forgiveness is, what it means for you, and how you can implement it in your life. Learn how to move forward, keeping wonderful relationships healthy, and about how and when to let go of toxic relationships.

Forgiveness:

A Brief Insight into Its Role in My Life

Forgiveness is something I've engaged in my whole life and continue to practice. When I was young, I did forgiveness, and I also didn't do forgiveness. I said I was sorry when I needed to, apologized, and even accepted apologies from others. What I didn't realize is that many times, I was "left wanting." I was still left feeling bad, rejected, even mad at the recall of a past experience. Many times, I adhered to the notion, "Forgive, but never forget."

I was religious for a lot of my life, but I now consider myself to be spiritual; my faith resides in LOVE. (I go deeper into the whole LOVE thing in the following chapters.) I mention this because part of the forgiveness I had to do was around religion and church. I learned about forgiveness in church—about how Jesus forgave, how God forgives us, and how we are supposed to forgive others. School teachers, my parents, people on TV, and friends all had something to say about apologizing and "forgiving" another person. I heard the words and the stories over and over, but what I witnessed and experienced was very different. The words did not match the actions.

I heard and saw people apologize, then do the same thing again and/or experience the person on the other side of the apology still being mad. It seemed as though neither side was any further ahead.

I had some frustrating and infuriating experiences in life and allowed them to affect me to my core. I allowed people and situations to dictate my emotions and well-being, not only in the moment but also for *many* "moments" to follow. The tension and turmoil with want-to-be-friends, friends, family, coworkers, in-laws, perfect strangers, and myself were never fully resolved because they would continue to rear their heads and wreak havoc whenever the opportunity presented itself.

Before I started my pursuit of healing and discovering all the modalities I now know, there was always something about forgiveness that echoed within me. On some level, I *knew* that forgiveness required a softening of the heart, a different way of thinking with the mind, and a different way of behaving within any relationship. The hard part was that I consciously knew this, but I had yet to figure out the whole unconscious part of it. That was the part that changed my life.

Once I figured out that almost all of our behaviors are based in beliefs—and that our beliefs and behaviors manifest from mostly old, but some new, information stored within our unconscious—a whole new world of chaos, opportunity, and the possibility for growth and true well-being was illuminated. I had a lot of work to do within myself. I knew I wanted to be different and experience the world around me differently. I was willing to do the work because I was no longer willing to experience life as I was experiencing it. I wanted more happiness, joy, calm, LOVE, and fulfillment.

I was introduced to hypnotherapy and neuro-linguistic programming (NLP). I saw a practitioner who was able to help me truly let go of the burdens I was carrying by holding on to the past, or at least ideas of and about the past. I saw how I was the one continuing to cause my own grief by what I thought about, how I thought about it, and how that all manifested in my current experiences. I was told, and then finally learned, that I was the only one who could free myself—no one else could do it. This was my sole responsibility, with help and guidance, of course, but it was up to me to let go of, heal from, and move through. Let me tell you, at times, it was so damn hard. But I did it, and I still do. (In the chapter "Forgiveness: A Speech That Found Its Way into This Book," I mention just a few of the things I've worked through in my life.)

There was no way I was going to allow other people, things, situations, and/or experiences to dictate the way I felt, thought, behaved, or existed in *my* life. I realized that I got to decide all of that for *myself*.

Forgiveness is something that is now ingrained in my being. Actually, quite literally—I have the Kanji symbols for forgiveness tattooed on the front side of my shoulders. If that's not a good reminder, I don't know what is! There are times that forgiveness seems more difficult than others, but I know the payoff for doing the work, so I do it with an open heart and gratitude.

In the following pages, I'm going to do my best to present a case for forgiveness. This book talks about what I am calling "pragmatic forgiveness." I think of pragmatic forgiveness as something that is as basic, dynamic, and profound as eating. It is not religiously based and is meant for anyone, with or without a religious or spiritual base. It's about letting go of the toxic and detrimental beliefs, thoughts, and trapped difficult emotions so you can engage more joy, happiness, well-being, and LOVE. A little caveat here, I refrain from using the term "negative emotions" because all of our emotions are essential and not one of them is negative, they are sometimes just difficult. If we view any of our emotions as negative, then we are telling ourselves that it's not okay to have them or feel them—feeling all of our emotions is exactly what we need to do to navigate them and heal through the tough ones.

I will provide you with essential information as to how you may have gotten to where you are and how you may be able to move forward. I offer many insights into how to look at forgiveness for what it truly means and how to apply and implement it for the sake of your healthiest well-being.

<u>Forgiveness is a practice.</u> It's about pursuing freedom, well-being, joy, happiness, and LOVE. It is absolutely a journey, but it has no finite destination. Forgiveness is about healing your own heart and mind—sometimes others benefit from it; sometimes they do not—and it's about not being attached to that outcome.

Forgiveness is about looking into the limitations that you've placed on yourself or allowed another to place on you and then freeing yourself from any limitations. Forgiveness helps you to learn, grow, evolve, experience more peace, and truly heal.

Some are teachers to you, and some are teachers for you.

—Melissa Reese

Forgiveness:

It Is Yours to Create

F orgiveness has been a big part of my journey. The pursuit of forgiveness is continuous, maybe not with the same people, but life always has something and someone new. In the following pages, I offer my insights on what I believe forgiveness to be, what it entails, and what it has to offer each and every soul.

Forgiveness and how we do it are not lightweight concepts. My words only scratch the surface of the profoundness that forgiveness is, that forgiveness stands for, and that forgiveness presupposes. If you think about it, if forgiveness did not exist, there would be either absolutely no imperfection or absolute perfection. There would be no fear and only LOVE. LOVE is forgiveness and never holds on to anger, sadness, fear, guilt, hurt, grief, or any other difficult emotions. Yet we, as humans, have such a hard time conceptualizing that, thinking about that, or even forming established reasoning for that. There have been many studies on forgiveness, and the conclusions emphasize feelings of freedom and healing, specifically freedom from stress, freedom from burden, freedom from weight (physically and metaphorically), freedom from darkness, freedom from an "all-consuming feeling," and freedom from grief and struggle.

Forgiveness *presupposes* a lack of perfection, a lack of LOVE, a lack of happiness, a lack of congruency, and to a certain degree, a lack of understanding. Forgiveness is, in a way, a duality. We need it when we are not in a place of LOVE, and when we are in the place of LOVE, it ceases to exist; there's no longer a need for it. In LOVE, everything exists without judgment and without fear. Creation and destruction are actually one and the same; there is no separation of life and death because death is life. Things must fall away in order for there to be space for something new. New life is nourished by that which has perished. Every cell, every organism requires nourishment. Growth and change do not happen without some sort of death. Not like a sacrificial thing, but the death of a thought, idea, belief, or behavior—that sort of thing. And really, there is no such thing as death; it's all simply a transition and/or transformation.

The earth, our bodies, our minds, and our environment are constantly providing *checks and balances*. Each element within our environment influences and plays a role in how we think, feel, and behave. The elements include, but are not limited to, earth, wind, fire, water, metal, wood, and ether (meaning what is above us). When there is a lot of fire, what do we need to tame it? Wind? No, that perpetuates it. Metal? No, that melts into it. Wood? No, that burns in it. In this scenario, water is the key element needed to subdue this element that could get out of control.

Water is what tames the fire and, in this case, saves the other elements. Is it better to not have fire? No, the burned wood is what provides a clearing, and combined with the water, it provides nutrition for the new growth that will take place. Also, fire can allow us to melt metal to make the tools that help us navigate the physical world. In this instance, fire can be considered a transgression or an imperfection, but it is also an essential element in the balance of life. In another scenario, water could be the transgressor, wearing away at metal until it rusts or drowning out a tree until it collapses.

Either way, there is healing that comes from these actions. Iron comes from rust and goes back into the earth, and rotted wood also goes back into the earth, with both providing nutrients for future growth. Within all darkness, light exists. Where there is light, there is no darkness. The earth's pull is there to keep us grounded so that we do not float out into the ether, at least until we are in a different energy form. But even gravity gets a bad rap as we see our skin and other parts of our body sag to undesirable levels as we age.

Without individual perceptions of right, wrong, good, and bad, there would be no forgiveness; there would be no rectifying, no learning, no lessons, and no growth. Although our spirits need none of that, our humanness needs all of that. If we all just lived in the "domain of LOVE," forgiveness simply would not exist; there would be no need. We humans need imperfection to notice perfection, we need wrong to know right, and we need to be able to forgive to know how to create the concepts and feelings of wholeness and LOVE.

The outcome of forgiveness is something beautiful, something pure, and something fulfilling. It is free of judgment and full of integrity, happiness, strength, and empowerment. Remember, it is a process. The experience of the fire and putting it out is what is needed to really experience growth. Forgiveness is something that provides freedom. It provides sanctity, security, and the feeling of health and well-being.

When we forgive ourselves, other people, and things, we allow ourselves to be free of limitations and negativity within us and outside of us. We can then feel freedom: freedom from those things that have the potential to hold us back from being who we want to be, from doing what we want to do, and from having what we want to have. Only you can make the choice to forgive (yourself and others). In that forgiveness, only you can choose to employ happiness, contentment, fulfillment, empowerment, courage, and whatever other wonderful way of being you want to add in here. It is all up to you as an individual. You have that power!

Forgiveness doesn't mean you are excusing the crime; it just means you are no longer willing to be the victim.

—*Unknown*

Forgiveness:

An Introduction and Foundation

In the last section, I dropped the word *LOVE*—a lot. I write it in all caps because I'm not talking about human love; I am talking about the "domain," space, place, inherent, eternal existence of LOVE. I'm also talking about the pure feeling, expression, and knowing of LOVE. I know there to be only LOVE and fear; everything is a by-product of one or the other. If you feel judgment, anger, hurt, guilt, grief, anxiousness, (insert your difficult emotion here), you are in fear. Recognizing this is not about fault or blame, just a "heads-up." As humans we simply experience these emotions, but a momentary experience of them versus a continuous experience of them is very different. Fear seems to be our default mode as humans; we seem to need to be consistently reminded of LOVE and brought back to LOVE.

When in LOVE, everything just is. There is no delineation of anger, grief, shame, fear, joy, or happiness—it is simply not needed. Everything is seen as equal when in LOVE. All the "positive" and "difficult" emotions exist in LOVE, but there is no difference. Fear, however, seems to constantly need to figure things out—dissect, scrutinize, criticize, judge, point out, separate, and so forth—but not LOVE. Nope, LOVE does none of that; it just does LOVE. LOVE knows all the "ugly" and the "beauty"—they are just the same.

There are many studies out there looking at LOVE and hate, fear, and shame. The conclusion of all is that LOVE is a higher vibration, it is a connecting vibration, and it is a vibration that provides healing.

Our minds are mighty, and our brain health influences the might of our minds. Also, we have multiple brains that make up our "minds." Each of us has a brain in the head, a brain in the heart, and a brain in the gut. When any of these are out of whack, our minds are out of whack. This is why mental, emotional, and physical health are all equally important. What you eat, what you read, what you watch, and what you engage in all matter, so very much. Everything carries a vibration, and if we consistently engage with and bring in lower vibrations, we set ourselves up to get out of whack. This is where being mindful comes in and where we can more consciously choose higher-vibrating things that keep us closer to LOVE and even in LOVE. Awareness is a key component of starting, creating, and achieving anything. Good thing you're reading this book—you're already becoming more aware and setting yourself up to invite more LOVE into your life!

LOVE is all the emotions and feelings anyone could ever experience but without any judgment or discernment. As previously mentioned, fear is not this. I also mentioned the might of our minds; this might can pull from LOVE or fear and work really well from either domain. The domain we choose to pull from is the reality we create and then live in. Our brains and our minds have no real concept of past, present, or future—only our thoughts and beliefs do. Our thoughts, and the beliefs we hold around those thoughts, are what create our present experiences. The present is moment to moment and leaves as quickly as it enters; the continuation of the present is determined by what we hold in our focus.

If a thought lands in our minds and stays for even a short stint, it can be the catalyst that creates our present experience, even though it may not actually be happening. Memories have feelings and emotions attached to them, so when we bring them up and hold them in our minds, we have a reaction or response to them. Time is a construct we've made up, and our minds do not adhere to it. With zero regard for time, the mind determines our present state—left unattended or to its own devices, this can be good or bad, depending on how you feel about what you've got stored in your memory database. The same goes for creating the future.

We create the future based on how we feel about our past and present. If we don't feel good about the past, the present typically isn't so great, and neither is the perceived future. Sometimes we create wonderful daydreams and fantasies that can positively affect our present state, but then we get snapped back to our "real" present state, and there goes the feel-good. By the way, this is how you know you have some work to do. This is how you know your default is fear and not LOVE. When in LOVE, your past, present, and future bring high vibrations and good feelings. The only time they wouldn't is if something actually seems like it sucks in your present state—like a hammer hitting your finger or some other crappy thing—but then you remember that you don't have to "play into the suck," and then it's all good again.

Our thoughts can greatly influence our beliefs. (Yes, on occasion, we do just have a fleeting thought, no biggie, but this is less common.) Our beliefs affect how we feel about our thoughts, and that determines our behaviors, reactions, and responses. It typically goes in this order: thoughts (new and old), beliefs (emotional ties), behaviors. It can also be that our limiting beliefs are what perpetuate our not-so-wonderful thoughts and behaviors. What I'm saying is that all we know is now—regardless of when the event we think about has taken place or will take place. Our beliefs about new or old information determine our responses and reactions, regardless of how truthful or valid the new or old information is. This is why forgiving your past is so imperative. Forgiveness gets you to LOVE, and that helps improve your overall well-being.

Have you ever become mad at or about something that was not true or even close to what you thought it was? How long was it until you "got over" it? How profoundly did that untrue incident affect you?

Now, did anything happen after that event that was similar and, in fact, true? (Take time to think about these next questions.) Did it involve the same people? What was your reaction to the event? Was it less intense than with the untrue event, of the same intensity, or more intense? If your reaction was the same or more intense, forgiveness might be something you want to look into.

Many of us seek freedom from the difficult emotions that make us feel defeated or not in control, but how is this freedom actually achieved? Where do we start, and how can we heal as quickly as possible to experience the freedom we so desire? The answer is **forgiveness**. Forgiveness is one pursuit in the continuous journey of life. It is a pursuit that has many different roads; some are short and lead directly to the destination, and others have yet to be forged, let alone paved. Forgiveness is a choice and a decision. It can take a long time to think about, but it can be implemented or achieved instantaneously.

Forgiveness, I believe, starts in the womb. We feel, sense, and experience almost everything our mothers experience and all other things around us. There are differing ideas on how many senses we really have, how we use them, and how we experience them, but basic science says we have only five senses: touch, taste, smell, sound, and sight. However, quantum physics and noetic[1] sciences have found that we have more than five senses. If learning more about quantum physics and noetic sciences is of interest to you, please do research on this. There is a link to a reference list in the back of this book and on my website. For now, I will keep it simple and limit the discussion to the idea of the senses as comprising touch, taste, smell, hearing, and seeing.

We do not interpret situations, people, or things the same way as our mothers do or as others around us do, yet we still have the experiences. As we have those experiences and develop our senses, we have physical feelings and emotions. We may not understand them, but we do experience them. A three-week-old

---

1 Noetics is a branch of metaphysical philosophy concerned with the study of mind and intellect. It is a multidisciplinary field that brings objective scientific tools and techniques together with subjective inner knowing to study the full range of human experiences.

baby does not have the ability to explain its emotions as it sits in a soiled diaper, but it does have the ability to cry. We can only interpret this cry with the labels we know. We can only *assume* that the baby feels "uncomfortable," "mad," "scared," "frustrated," and so forth. It may be feeling all those things and some things we have no label for.

There are times when it is difficult to put our thoughts and emotions into words. Even when we are able to label them, it is really only within us that we truly understand what the label (word) represents. Another person may use the same word to label a thought or emotion, but he or she may internalize what it means completely differently than we did. As we experience (through our senses) different feelings and emotions, we start to create our neural networks—think of them as our databases.

The databases store everything old and everything new: all the old labels and all the new labels. Each network has different categories built in. The categories are created much like a filing system. This filing system and all the memories and feelings that are contained within it are stored in our unconscious (subconscious) minds, our brains, and the cells in our bodies. (I go further into this later on.) Things that are the same, or very similar, get filed together, and subset folders are created for each event in which we experience similar emotions. If you've ever worked with a filing cabinet, think of it kind of like that. Or if you are one of those highly organized people that has all their Apps. on their smart phone in designated folders based on subject or similarity, then think of it kind of like that.

Now, our neural networks are built from our senses and include experiences, thoughts, ideas, beliefs, and emotions. This is how we filter our world and how we create what we know reality to be. In the womb, and until we develop vocabulary, we do not have the words to label the emotions we are feeling, but we are still feeling them and filing them in different categories. Once we have labels (words) for the emotions we have been feeling, we tend to generalize. Those generalizations go into the categories we have already created, and we start to create new ones. For instance, anger and frustration are similar enough that they get filed into the same category. From these categories, we start to develop new ideas, thoughts, and beliefs. Words and labels continuously take on new meaning as we grow and have new experiences.

As I mentioned, each category is created by filtering information, and we can only filter new information using what we have already experienced or created to be "true." At a young age, our filters are almost nonexistent; we are simply looking through a clear glass window. As we live our lives, we create filters based on all of the events and emotions we have experienced. Different events and emotions can create ideal filters or not-so-ideal filters.

Let me start to explain this with a continuation of the aforementioned example of the clear window. The clear window lets everything in—all the light, all the possible visibility—while still protecting us from much of the outside elements, but there's still a lot coming in. We can observe and be observed, and then we notice that clear window allows for everything to be seen—so we start the protection process. We add filters and blockers. The filters can start with simply adding tinting or UV protection to the window. Then, screens are added for if or when we want to open the window—we get the fresh air without certain parts of nature coming in through the window. For more privacy, we add shades or blinds, then maybe curtains. Then, outside, we install hanging shades. By now, the window is tinted, screens are attached to the window, shades or blinds and curtains cover the inside of the window, and hanging shades cover the outside. If all of these are closed at once, what's getting in? Then there are some that just go for the complete block out with the ever-so-thrifty aluminum foil—definitely no light or observation coming in or going out.

Some of our filters are chosen, and others were handed to us to use without question. Our friends, family, religion, disabilities, and abilities can very quickly determine how and what we "see." Think of it this way: You and three other people can be taking a picture of the same thing, and all three pictures turn out differently. Maybe one is a "selfie," one was taken by some nice person standing around you, one was taken from the right side, and one was taken from the left side. Whether using a cell phone or a regular camera, the lens, filters, and timing; the length of your arm; and extra equipment all make a difference in what is captured in the photo. You look at all three pictures taken, they are somewhat the same because they include mostly the same elements, just expressed differently. All the above mentioned variables, plus timing, create small and significant variations. And let's face it, we all have that one picture out of all of them that is our favorite because, well, we look good in that one. Just like a camera, the picture we create of our world and our reality is altered by "filters" and "lenses," whatever they may be. How do your filters and lenses affect the "pictures" of your life and your views on life, reality, and the world around you?

We operate based on very early perceptions of experiences and emotions and create our own databases for deciphering our world. This is great for learning and navigating, but when we hold on to old experiences as absolutely true, we alter the filters that determine how we perceive our world. As we gain new knowledge, it is most beneficial to take a look at some of the beliefs or viewpoints we already have filtered and stored in our databases to see how they match up to our new experiences.

For just a moment, think about when you've looked back at an old photo; you see things you didn't see before and realize things about it you didn't realize before. How you feel about the photo now is not the same as how you felt about the photo when you first saw it or even when it was taken. If we all looked into the internal photo database of our lives on a regular basis, we could get rid of so much past hurt, confusion, and misinterpretation that we tend to carry with us into our adult lives.

From a very young age, we choose and decide which thoughts become beliefs and which ones we allow to be simply fleeting thoughts and ideas. Not all thoughts become a belief; some are just thoughts in the moment. What matters is the impact of the thought and its recurrence. The more information we collect, the more we categorize. Some people make more categories than others, and these categories are what we pull from to operate our lives and create the world around us.

I hope I have helped make it clear that we have the ability to choose and decipher from a very young age. *We do not necessarily have the knowledge, skill, or wisdom to implement or fully understand what we have chosen to decide or believe.* We do what we feel or understand to be the best for us at that time. This is why it is important to do housecleaning of our databases as we get older. We usually store stuff that is not applicable any longer or does not serve us according to what we deem best because it is no longer best.

As we integrate (internalize) the lessons and knowledge from our lives, we get to decipher what is best for us; this concept is something we continuously figure out. By the way, age does not seem to play a critical role in how we decipher and choose what is best for us, although it is a factor. What we deem best seems to depend on how much we are in tune with our intuition (our inner-loving-knowing); how long we stay connected to our intuition; and how much we consider others' opinions, beliefs, and experiences when creating our own.

This is a very small glimpse into how we each create our own reality. Forgiveness can be the start of altering your state of being, thinking, and feeling. It is what you use to decide what filters are most beneficial to you. Forgiveness helps you get the best pictures of your world and the world around you.

Perception is everything. What one person sees, another may not or may see in a very different way. Our filters are what determine our world and our realities. Five hundred people can watch the exact same thing happen, and all five hundred will recall a different rendition of the event. All will have internalized it and what it meant to them differently. All will tell about what happened as if it were true, real, and exact—because for *them*, it was. How can this be?

We all take in only so much information at a time; it is impossible for us to take in everything happening and store every single movement, sound, color, and feeling all at once. What you focus on determines what information comes in. How tired you are determines how much information comes in. How you feel and what you believe also determine how much and what type of information comes in. If a person is blind, deaf, in a wheelchair, on crutches, or on drugs, this will determine how information is filtered. The number of people you are around, the type of people you are around, and so on and so forth all play a huge role in how your filter is working to create information that gets stored in your database.

Something fun: Ask your friends, family, or coworkers—really anyone—to use five words that describe LOVE. Basically, the list should consist of five words that equal LOVE to them. See how the five words from each person's list match up to your list. If you want to go a bit further, see how many lists, if any, have the same five descriptive words. Have people work quietly and individually to do this task. If you want to get a little more personal and have fun with this game, have people list five words that equal the word *sex* to them. It can be any five words that come to mind when they think of sex. By the way, this exercise has been done by Dr. Matthew James, a master practitioner trainer of NLP (neuro-linguistic programming) and doctor of psychology. In his training sessions, and in his thirty-three years of teaching, he has only found two people who created identical lists with all five words matching. We all internalize the meanings of words uniquely. Do you see how, similarly, we also internalize relationships and situations uniquely? This uniqueness, at the core, is where miscommunication is conceived—and it's also what provides the biggest and best opportunities for learning, growing, understanding, respecting, and appreciating.

I briefly mentioned "conditions" that determine and alter our filters. These can also be the exact things that affect our situational ability to be in LOVE or even ready to pursue forgiveness. Certain conditions affect our lives from the beginning—built-in filters, if you will. Any person who is born as or becomes blind, deaf, or paralyzed; loses the sense of taste; loses the sense of smell; has an intellectual limitation; or is an absolute "genius," for example, will have altered senses, filters, and experiences. This alteration is neither good nor bad; it merely creates a completely different way of viewing and experiencing the world. I bring this up because I want to emphasize that sometimes we have more to forgive—right from day one—than we are aware of.

Many times, we come to accept what has been dealt to us. This acceptance is wonderful. However, does such acceptance include forgiveness within it, or do we have to remind ourselves to accept what we have been dealt on a daily basis? Acceptance of a person, thing, or event does not mean forgiveness has been given. Reflect on this. What comes up? If a feeling of pity or feeling sorry for yourself or someone else is present, this is limiting and automatically implies "victim mode." Victim mode is the opposite of forgiveness. In a subsequent chapter, I will get deeper into being a victim versus what I call the "experiencer." For now, I will sum it up: a victim dwells, and an experiencer creates and moves forward with LOVE and freedom.

Our filters can change from moment to moment and day to day. Take some time to think about these next questions. Have you ever seen a movie more than once? During the second viewing, did you hear, see, and feel things you did not notice during the first viewing? Where did you watch it the first time? What mood were you in? What were your expectations? Who were you with? Were you sober or not?

Try reading a book (this one, for example) for a second or even third time. I bet you will get more and more from it each time. Have a conversation with someone, and if a topic comes up that you have talked about before, notice *anything* that may be different about it this time.

Our perceptions of things, people, and events will change with time, as well as with repetition, and sometimes the change is immediate. Have you ever found out a piece of information about someone that caused you, in that instant, to feel differently about the person? Your perceptions of your own behavior and other people's behavior and the feedback you get are what form your reality. Your reality can determine what role a person, situation, or thing plays in your life. Each person's reality is unique. If the reality you have created is not working as well as you would like, you have all the power to create and implement a different one.

Each culture, religion, and person holds traditions, rituals, and ideologies believed, in the mind, to be true and right. When those things bump up against or challenge our own, we tend to defend or retreat, and sometimes, we feel anger or fear. This moment is the best time to forgive and let go. Do what you feel is right for you, and redirect your focus to the things and people who make you feel happy, purposeful, and fulfilled. Forgiveness is not for other people; it is for you. It is for your own healing and well-being and for you to create a world you deem acceptable. You get to determine who and what is in *your* world—without judgment and without grudge or regret.

Who's wrong and who's right? That's for you to decide—maybe you're both right; maybe you're both wrong. Either way, when both are equal, that's LOVE. Just because you do not think you did anything wrong does not mean someone else thinks the same. Like I mentioned, we are all creating from day one. We have all created our own moral compasses, our own codes of ethics, and our own ideas of what is right and wrong. I am not going to lie: this can be a frustrating thought and concept, but it is one that will help you in starting your journey into the realm of forgiveness and onto a path of happiness and freedom.

Empower yourself to cultivate and create happiness, which forgiveness will help perpetuate. This kind of happiness is your way of being, way of doing, and the filter through which you look at life. I am talking about self-actualized happiness; it is the opposite of moment-to-moment experiences and of happiness brought to you or co-created by another outside of you. This kind of happiness means that no matter what happens, you find the "glass half-full" and gratitude for what *is* and was instead of what wasn't and what is not. All experiences offer an opportunity—a lesson, something to learn, a way to more quickly smile. The happiness that is *you* (fully integrated within your being) is where you operate from. Sure, food, money, sex, alcohol/drugs, and other things can afford temporary perceptions of happiness, but all that temporary happiness does is keep you searching—pacified momentarily, but not long after, you are left wanting. Forgiveness heals. It creates and

cultivates a more permanent happiness every ...
you experience it. Forgiveness gets you to LOVE, and
when in LOVE, you are never left wanting.

*Forgiveness does not excuse their behavior;
forgiveness prevents their behavior from
destroying your heart.*

—Unknown

*A teacher asked, 'What is forgiveness?' A little
girl responded, 'It is the wonderful smell that
a flower gives when it is being crushed.'*

—Unknown

Forgiveness:

The Purpose

Forgiveness is not necessarily a religious thing. There is no dogma—not even a right or wrong way to forgive. Forgiveness is a way of being, living, thinking, and behaving. It is about releasing and freeing yourself from resentment, fear, anger, sadness, guilt, or any other emotion causing you grief, unhappiness, or pain. Knowing forgiveness is about knowing and creating happiness, contentment, freedom, and a sense of calm. It is the ability to harness much more control over your emotional, mental, and physical well-being. It is being able to look at a person, thing, or situation and feel delighted that you have freed yourself from the "cage" or "circus." It is that moment when you know the feeling of freedom in your heart, mind, and body despite who or what is around you. It is knowing that *you* are the one in control of your well-being. It is seeing anything in your past with a total feeling of neutrality or LOVE and feeling gratitude for where it brought you—giving you the opportunity to heal and grow.

When we are living in a place of forgiveness for ourselves and other people, we are more easily able to navigate and even better control how we feel, think, live, and behave. When in a place of forgiveness, we embody power and strength. In the words of Mahatma Gandhi, "The weak can never forgive; forgiveness is the attribute of the strong." Forgiveness is a responsibility to yourself.

What is this thing called forgiveness, and what exactly does it encompass? Forgiveness is not about saying you're sorry or about making sure somebody else knows and feels the wrong he or she has done; it is not about acknowledging any of that at all. Forgiveness *is* about you acknowledging how another person's behavior, thoughts, or emotions affected you and loving yourself enough to say, "I am ready to let that go." *Self-forgiveness* is about you acknowledging times of a lack of responsibility to yourself and then redeciding and figuring out what you want to do differently to benefit your overall well-being.

When it comes down to it, we are the only ones capable of harboring our own feelings; no one else can harbor our feelings for us. Forgiveness is not about saying that another person's behavior, actions, thoughts, feelings, or emotions are OK. We each decipher and determine what is good, bad, or OK. What is good and bad to us is not necessarily good or bad to another. It is about allowing that other person to simply be who he or she is and do what he or she does without you being tied in with or attached to those things in any way. It is about acknowledging that another person is responsible only for him- or herself. You are responsible for your own physical, mental, and emotional well-being.

Have you ever wanted something for someone else so badly, only to be disappointed when the outcome was not what you wanted? Maybe the behavior looks promising for a short while but fades quickly or is only intermittent. A person cannot simply behave for the sake of another. How a person behaves has to be a personal decision, and a benefit must be experienced from it (the behavior) in order for other people to experience the benefit as well. When you want something more for someone else and are attached to the outcome, it sets you up for failure and has a tendency to make the other person feel the same—sometimes, the other person may not even care at all. Either way, this setup begins a cycle of feeling let down, resentful, and angry and a pattern of being "left wanting." Although I believe there is no failure, only feedback, it is not really feedback if the pattern (behavior) never changes. Most of us have heard the saying, "The definition of insanity is doing the same thing over and over expecting different results."

We are each in charge of our own thoughts, behaviors, and emotions. Forgiveness is about being completely in charge, taking full responsibility for and of yourself, making a decision, creating a template that you want to live by, creating your own world that you want to live in, and abiding by what you have created for the sake of *you*. Creating is about deciphering, not judging. Forgiveness is about not allowing another person to live rent-free in your heart and head, disrupting your mind. It is about not allowing another person to affect you in any negative or unwarranted way and healing the past. You get to be free of judgment toward yourself and another person, not expecting the other person to behave, think, or be a different way. We each have control over ourselves. We cannot control any of the aforementioned things in another person. It is beyond futile to continue to try or think it is even a possibility.

A lack of forgiveness, including self-forgiveness, becomes a crutch. This crutch consists of all the people, reasons, and excuses that have grown and are festering in the void, and only forgiveness will allow you the freedom to completely transcend any and all limitations. Only forgiveness will allow you to take the responsibility that you will need to create the life you want. The world happens around us, and our response to it determines how it affects us. If we are not careful with our boundaries, nonbeneficial things can infiltrate them. This infiltration can affect whether we respond or react. Create your boundaries, know what they are, and stay true to them. Learn and know when you need to say *no* and when you need to say *yes*—understand your reasoning behind those words. These boundaries give you the ability to respond appropriately by being responsible for your own thoughts, emotions, and behaviors. Empowering yourself with this knowledge is the key to being successful in life. To me, it is the key to fulfilling your purpose, whatever that may be. (You can also check out my other book, *The Pursuit of More*, for further info on this.)

What is your purpose? Is it to teach; to simply be kind to yourself and others; to write, paint, dance, or garden; to help in some field of medicine; or something else? It is not up to another to determine your purpose; it is up to you to figure it out for yourself. When we live another's purpose, we tend to live in a place of lacking, feeling unfulfilled, resentful, and maybe even angry or afraid. Our parents, teachers, and mentors are not meant to mold us into carbon copies of what they think and believe or how they behave. They are meant to be examples that we pull the best from, leaving the rest. What worked to make one person successful may not work for you because you are not made the same way. Adapting information to you instead of adapting yourself to it is how you find, implement, and create your purpose. When you have your purpose, you have the foundation set for staying true to you, and you are better equipped for success. And by the way, you may have, more than one purpose. Any purpose is something you have felt called to do or feel called to do. It is a feeling brought to life with well-intentioned action. Some purposes feel bigger than others, but they all matter. There are lessons, joys, and happinesses that come with all purposes.

We are meant to be happy. We are created for happiness. How do I know this? Because we are equipped with chemical receptors for happiness. Yes, we are equipped for other chemical reactions, and the reactions we have the most become what our bodies' receptors are most ready for. Receptors are like key holes, and our chemicals are the keys. It is imperative to develop the receptors that the "happy" keys fit into. This is where you get to choose and decide what chemical reactions you want taking place most often and what you want your body to be most ready for. (If you would like more information on our creation of chemicals and how deeply these chemicals affect us, watch the movie *What the Bleep Do We Know?* or read these books: *Molecules of Emotion* by Candace Pert and *The Honeymoon Effect* by Bruce Lipton. If you are living another's purpose, feeling unsuccessful, or feeling lost, start with forgiving yourself and then anyone else you think may be keeping you from the life you want. The more you forgive, the more "happy" chemicals you release, which will set your body up for future success and well-being.

Forgiveness increases and creates healthy patterns of thinking, doing, and being in our lives. If your physical, mental, and emotional well-being are "off" or less than what you deem good and your happiness is not increasing despite doing the forgiveness, maybe look at *what* it is you are forgiving. Is there something you are missing? Have you made sure to forgive all the aspects and people involved? Sometimes you need to forgive the person who was part of the situation and all the things and people involved. Could it be time to let go of that person, thing, or situation? You get to decide what is best for you, and if there are any feelings of guilt, forgive yourself.

It is impossible to be a person of strength if you do not care for yourself first. If you focus on other people first, you deplete yourself and have nothing to use to build within you. If you are unable to build within yourself, how long are you going to last taking care of others first? Not long. It is futile and, I will go as far as to say, irresponsible to not take care of yourself first. The simplest yet most powerful metaphor for this is one you may have heard but is worth repeating. On a plane, they direct you to put the oxygen mask on yourself first; then, if the person next to you needs help, you are able to help that person. How can you help anyone around you if you are dead? And to take it a step further, if you are dead, you actually become a burden to all the others because now they have to figure out what to do with you. Give yourself the "oxygen" you need in order to be able to help those who want it. Remember, you may think another person needs help, but that person has the right to refuse it. Keep helping yourself, and only focus on those who are not only reaching out but also using the help you are offering. If you can build beneficial patterns within yourself, you actually have more to give to others, if you so choose. Therefore, forgive for the sake of yourself, not for another. Let go for the sake of yourself, not for another. Learn for the sake of yourself, not for another.

Forgiveness:

It Is Yours to Engage

If you think about forgiveness, it has many facets. There are many ways to forgive. What you do after you have forgiven is up to you. You either forgive and move forward with the person or people or forgive and move forward without that person or people. Just because we forgive someone does not mean we *need* to have any sort of relationship with the person or even like him or her. You can "nothing" people—you don't wish them harm, you don't like or love them, but you also do not dislike them; you wish them only peace, LOVE, and healing, and you simply feel content within yourself. You decide what outcome is best for your well-being. A forgiving release means there are no longer any feelings of dislike, in conjunction with a *true* feeling of not wanting anything bad to happen to the person/people. Forgiving yourself, on the other hand, means you get to establish a *better* feeling about *you*: who you are, what you do, and how you internalize that. This makes it easier to decipher who and what get to stay and go in your life in order to create the happiness and love you are meant for.

Some of the definitions of forgiveness describe it as a pardon, an absolution, mercy, a reprieve, a wiping of the slate clean, or an excusing. You get to be the one who decides what forgiveness is to you and for you. Are you pardoning, excusing, or letting go? If so, what are you pardoning excusing, or letting go? Are you showing mercy? If so, to whom? I hope the answers to these questions are "myself." You are not pardoning or excusing the other person's behavior. You are pardoning or excusing the results. It is about acknowledging, excusing, and pardoning your own feelings, apprehensions, anger, and limitations that can and do tend to keep people in a victim or martyr state. When people are in those states of being, they are not in control of being the creator of their own thoughts and feelings. They tend to feel a lack of purpose and are not in control of being able to feel empowered, happy, content, or whatever other wonderful adjective you want to put in there. Why is this? Because they are still harboring negativity in some way, and that is what creates the limitations.

There is a deep, profound gift that forgiveness provides to each of us. People who forgive experience a shift or change for the better. We can look at forgiveness as the ultimate wonderment and gift. We bestow it upon ourselves. By receiving this gift, we allow for dramatic change in our perception of our unique worlds and how we live in them. You determine the courage you create and feel with each process of forgiveness. You give yourself the continued gift of encouragement. Thus, you allow yourself to feel and experience love, fulfillment, contentment, and happiness. This allowance determines almost your entire outlook on life.

If you think about it, without forgiveness, as human beings, all we tend to know is right or wrong (determined by our own filters), hurt feelings, the feelings of not being heard or not being good enough, grudges, tit-for-tat reasoning, the feeling of unfairness, and the unfulfilled need for fairness. If you look at the amount of imbalance in your or another person's life, you can see the absence of forgiveness. It is unbelievable that somebody would choose not to embrace this thing, this concept, this energy, this amazing gift. It is literally life-changing—physiologically, energetically, mentally, and emotionally. It is amazing what forgiveness can conquer, cure, and open up.

Forgiveness is not for the other person to understand. Many times, when we forgive, we have to let go. Sometimes the other person may feel more hurt, but that is not for you to "fix"; it is for the other person to rectify within him- or herself. If you have forgiven and then talked to, tried to reason with, or even put up with a person, thing, or situation and the result continues to be less than pleasant, it is probably time to let go. Sometimes, time heals a relationship, and sometimes, it does not. One person can forgive, and the other may choose not to. You cannot make another person do the work. If you have done it and the other has not, you have to decide if you are OK with that person or the situation or not. Forgiveness is also about boundaries. Toxic is toxic, blood relation or not. Even Superman has kryptonite. You can only be around your "kryptonite" for so long before it takes you down.

When you forgive, you are setting a boundary for yourself of what is acceptable behavior. How you want to be liked, loved, and cared for is up to you. After all, we are the ones who teach others what is OK by what we "let fly." We teach people how to love and treat us. If you continue to allow people to do the same things and find yourself forgiving the same people or person for the same things, what are you learning, and what are you teaching? Forgive as much as you need and want to. If forgiving becomes a pattern with the same types of situations and people, you may need to take a step back and evaluate what you may need to forgive within yourself. This may be an opportunity presenting itself, showing you it's time to heal and build your self-worth. When you feel you are in a place of forgiveness with a person, situation, or thing, decide if the person, situation, or thing is worth moving forward with. Is it time to say goodbye? Goodbye can be permanent or for a designated amount of time. Sometimes we need space. Creating space allows for more freedom, and your freedom allows you to wander and gather exactly what you need to determine and create the most beneficial reality for yourself and the world around you. If you've allowed your space to be filled by others, for others, you must clean that space out. Create space that only you place things in—ideas, feelings, memories, LOVE, and so forth.

Forgiveness:

Conscious versus Unconscious (Subconscious)

So you want to be able to forgive, let go, feel freedom, and be happy. You tell yourself you are ready. Maybe you even go through the process, or maybe you just decide you feel like it is all done. You feel good and go about your life. At some later point, a person, situation, or thing is brought up, and all of a sudden, it changes your mood or behavior or becomes the main topic of discussion over the next day or longer. What happened? You decided to forgive, let go, and move on, or so you thought. So what's going on? When we make a decision, we are dealing with two minds. We have a conscious mind and an unconscious mind (some call it the subconscious). The conscious mind is our "goal-setter," and the unconscious mind is our "goal-getter." You have set your goal to forgive, yet it does not seem as though it fully worked.

Various studies have determined what percentages of our conscious and unconscious minds we use. These studies have found that the conscious mind makes up about 5 to 7 percent of who we are, what we think about, and how we do things. The unconscious mind makes up about 93 to 95 percent of who we are and how we do things. Think about that for a minute. That is a huge difference.

The unconscious mind's job is to keep us safe and take the path of least resistance. It helps our respiratory, circulatory, digestive, and other systems keep us alive and functioning. The unconscious mind also stores every memory and every experience we have ever had, according to our lenses and filters. If we were consciously aware of all of this going on at the same time, I'm pretty sure our heads would explode. OK, maybe not explode, but you can see that the conscious mind is only designed for things happening now or at any future time, including daydreaming and creating. I previously touched on this idea, and here I will go a bit further with it.

Think of your unconscious mind as a filing cabinet or a folder on your phone/computer. (You can also think if it as the aforementioned clear window that gets dirty and littered with various filters.) Let's keep going with this: A filing cabinet has drawers designated for specific files containing pieces of paper and folders. Items that are similar or go together get filed together in a specific order. On your smartphone, you can create folders in which to place similar apps—grouping them for the sake of condensing and/or organizing. You can also place the folders you create in a specific order to your liking, for either aesthetic purposes or ease of accessing specific apps. In these external scenarios, you have more control over your filing specifications; however, the unconscious mind does it according to chemical reactions, thoughts, beliefs, and behaviors—mostly without our conscious direction.

The conscious mind uses information from the unconscious when it needs that information to deal with or process the current experience. Think about a time when you were daydreaming. Were you thinking about a past event and making it different, or were you thinking about a future event and creating it? This brings me to another point: Have you noticed that when you pull a memory up and think about it, or daydream, you feel emotions as if that experience is happening in the moment? That sensation occurs because the unconscious mind has a timeline but not necessarily the ability to operate in the moment you are actually in if you are thinking about another time. What do I mean by this? The answer is a bit convoluted, but really read what I am saying; it is an important piece to being in control of your entire well-being.

Consider a scenario in which you are thinking about a promotion, an upcoming date, or maybe a fun trip you have planned. As you think about this future situation, you are probably feeling excited, hopeful, happy, and many other positive emotions. In this moment, in that imaginary time and space, you are feeling great. Then, you snap out of it and are back at your work desk or the kitchen table, with screaming kids running around. Those positive emotions stay for a short time until your new, in-the-moment emotions kick back in. Now, let's say you pull up a past memory, and you relive it as you think about it. That memory becomes the moment you are in, so the emotions tied to the memory are what you will experience, even if for just that moment. When you stop thinking about the memory, you are back in the current moment, able to experience *now* emotions.

Notice how long those "past" emotions stay in moments like these. Do they fade as quickly as the positive "future" emotions? Do they linger and stay longer than the future emotions? If they linger, this is a great indicator that some forgiveness work can be done. You want the positive emotions to always stay longer than the difficult. You want to be able to snap out of it and let your current state be that of beneficial emotion.

Also, when you pull up a memory that was put away, the memory may not be expressed in the present in the same way it was created back then. When your filters change, you view things differently. You had one filter in place when the past was happening, and you may find that you have a different filter in place now, when the past is being recalled. You may have liked or not liked the person, people, or situation when the memory was created, but you do or don't now. Pay attention to the emotions you experience when thinking about a memory or creating a daydream.

Sometimes, we are able to pull memories from the unconscious quickly, and other times, this recall is not so quick. Why is this? Well, like I said, the unconscious mind is tasked with keeping us safe. If there is something too big to deal with or a trauma is involved, the unconscious mind will have a very difficult time communicating with the conscious mind. This difficulty does not mean the information is lost. It means that we either do not have the coping mechanisms to deal with a memory at the given moment or we have created a faulty connection to the database. A faulty connection can be due to a head injury, drugs, alcohol, or illness. The thing is, I believe that you can always heal, on some level, faulty connection or not. You can implement forgiveness and reap the rewards, but you may have to be a bit more creative in how you navigate the process.

Like I said, the conscious mind is the goal-setter, and the unconscious mind is the goal-getter. Consciously, you have stated that you have forgiven. Then why is the person, situation, or thing still affecting you? There may be more pain to deal with than you are consciously able to think about or be aware of at the given moment. Sometimes, being ready and prepared to forgive is the first step. Then, the unconscious mind needs to be directed and guided through healing the past when in a meditative, hypnotic, or trance state in order to complete the process. I have a breathing technique that helps me do this, and I pair it with various healing processes. It took time to learn and implement this as a daily discipline. Before I learned how to do this on my own, I saw a hypnotherapist and neuro-linguistic programming (NLP) practitioner to help me. I needed help getting out of my own way. (By the way, sometimes I still do! I believe in forgiveness and doing the work, and I am human; sometimes I have to remember to get back to LOVE.)

At one point, my unconscious mind had so many old file folders and subset file folders attached to the original file folders that it, my unconscious, was a little messy and a bit overwhelming. I needed an unbiased, outside-of-me, nonfamily person to provide me with some new tools, like an eraser, shredder, garbage truck, or app. I also needed to be shown how the tools worked to reconstruct and redecide my filters and beliefs. I needed nonleading tools that I could use, when shown how to properly use them, to get rid of and delete files and folders or get better apps. *Nonleading* means you are doing the work; someone else simply shows you how to use the tools provided in the most beneficial and potent ways. There is a huge difference between suggesting and implanting. Never let anyone help you reconstruct and redecide your beliefs and filters—you decide the files, folders, and apps and their order. The help is only there for instruction on the tools, techniques, and processes.

Think about your phone or computer. Each app does something different. The apps were created to ease the process of accessing information and/or performing necessary tasks. Apps make the navigation of anything a bit simpler. Yes, sometimes people end up with way too many apps, and then organizing those is also a chore, but we could go down a huge rabbit hole with all that. Now, although applications were created to provide simplicity, shortcuts, and ease, they still have bugs and need to be updated periodically to stay compatible with upgraded software and hardware. An app is not just developed and then works perfectly forever, without any tweaks or changes—and the same goes for us. Sometimes we create things that need to be tweaked, changed, or just deleted.

Our brains work in specific ways to pattern things according to our morals, ethics, and character. The brain is always looking to pattern things in ways that benefit us. That is why we must decipher what is an illusion of benefit and what is really a benefit. Our hearts and minds know what our personal morals, ethics, and integrity are. When we are operating from a place other than that, we will tend to see different behaviors than what we *expect* from ourselves—our words and thoughts may not reflect our actions. These different, less optimal behaviors are what we need to go in and change.

In doing this work, I realized my unconscious was not purposely trying to hold me back or cause detriment—in fact, quite the opposite. It was taking the path of least resistance. The unconscious mind sticks to what it knows, to what it has been programmed to do. Offering up new tools with no instructions or new tools that *seem* more difficult to use can be overwhelming or create a bit of internal chaos. My unconscious mind only knew how to create more filters, files, and folders, instead of changing them or getting rid of them. It was using what it had previously stored as "good" information and the beneficial tools to do its best to keep me safe. Meanwhile, my conscious mind had other, opposite ideas and wanted to do things differently. I had goals I wanted to achieve. I wanted a better view through my window—really, I wanted to go outside to see more than just from my window.

The only way I could achieve these goals of forgiveness, freedom, and happiness was to go in and, with the help of the new tools, reconstruct my filters and files, rewire my difficult emotions away from negative memories, and create new neural networks that were more positive. When we have an experience, it creates a memory, and emotions are automatically attached to that memory. When "doing the work," you only work with the not-so-great memories, experiences, and emotions. You want to keep the good ones intact and thriving. Also, when you do the work of forgiving and letting go, you are not ever wiping your memory clean; you keep the memory, but you discard the difficult emotional charge attached to the memory. By allowing my unconscious mind to do this, I was able to create new paths of least resistance so that my unconscious mind could communicate more effectively and openly with my conscious mind.

I realized I could ditch many of my filters, files, folders, and apps; create new ones (if I wanted); and go outside my window. As I did the work, I found that I could safely navigate all that I saw outside my window, and I realized that I couldn't care less about who sees in my window. I got to choose which filters allowed me to best see the paths I wanted to continue on in my journey, and I still get to choose. I got rid of all the old, nonbeneficial, emotional networks that were tied to memories. I kept the memories but detached the difficult emotional charge, leaving room to input and create new, more beneficial feelings instead. Kryptonite will continue to appear in life, but knowing how to navigate around and safely away from it is the key.

By doing the work, I gave myself more options to deal and cope with anything new in a better, more beneficial way, whether it be similar to a past event or not. Now, I get to see the beauty that is beyond and navigate forward in the directions I deem most beneficial.

I want to be clear that I did not rewrite the memories. I just took the lessons and learnings needed to move forward and chose to look at the memories through a new or different filter. Now, when my conscious mind says, "I am ready to forgive" or "I am ready for a new goal," my unconscious mind is in agreement. It sounds something like this, "Hell yes, you've got this—go now; do it." They are in direct communication, ready to pursue the creation of the most beneficial life as I imagine it. I create the goal, and I am able to more easily take the steps I need to see the goal to fruition.

By the way, I still have times when I need resources outside of myself and consult someone else. I have come to learn about myself in such a way that I know when I have gone as far as I am going to go with self-observation and self-awareness. I have learned to recognize when it is time to call in someone I trust to help guide me past a limitation I created so that I can learn from it, move past it, and reap the benefits. Holistic practitioners and coaches exist for a reason. We can't do it all by ourselves. All the healing we do is only done by the self, but it sometimes takes the help of others to get us to that point where we are able to realize, understand, and allow ourselves to let go.

Forgiveness:

Associate to Disconnect

In this chapter, I go a little further into talking about the unconscious mind and the database that has all the files (memories) wired together with emotions. Here, I offer a different metaphor, as well as deeper information to tie together the importance of being able to deal with and navigate the process of freeing yourself from stored difficult emotions and setting yourself up to be in a place where you are truly able to forgive.

Consider a light-switch metaphor. Think of the switch itself as the memory and the wires as the emotional connection to that memory. Some memories are wonderful, but some not so much. When doing work to heal, we do not work *on* the wonderful memories but *with* them, using the wonderful memories to aid in filtering and eliminating the difficult emotions tied to the detrimental memories. You keep the wonderful memories hardwired to the main breaker.

I have already talked about how when we remember something, emotions tend to flood our minds and bodies, as if we were experiencing that particular (past) time in the present moment. The feelings that emerge are either welcomed or not. Either way, they make an appearance, even if only for a very short time. We have more control over some memories than others. Like I mentioned before, some memories can be retrieved instantly, whereas others can be more difficult to pull up. Memories affect us physiologically, and the physiological response to a memory also affects our health and well-being. The impact may or may not be beneficial. How wonderful would it be if, regardless of what memory came to mind, the physiological response would be beneficial, and you would be more in control of your emotions and behavior (maybe instead of your emotions and behavior controlling you)?

With forgiveness (and other techniques within neuro-linguistic programming [NLP] or hypnosis), you can make every memory beneficial. Here is how. When a memory comes to mind, pay attention to how you feel about it.

Is it creating happiness or not?

Is it creating calm or not?

Is it creating confidence, excitement, or anything else you deem beneficial?

If not, then it is time to cut and remove the emotional wires from the switch. So the memory stays, but the nonbeneficial response no longer exists. This benefits you because if there isn't a difficult emotional response, you won't release harmful[2] chemicals into your system and experience the less-than-beneficial feelings most of us dislike experiencing. Remember, you are only cutting power to the negative switches; the main breaker is what harnesses the beneficial emotions that power all positive switches.

The more you exercise the process of forgiveness around nonbeneficial memories, the more you are disconnecting the emotional wires attached to them. Therefore, each nonbeneficial memory loses its power over you, and you are left with even more control

2 The chemicals released when experiencing our difficult emotions are not harmful when experienced once in a while. When we experience them often and/or based on the past in conjunction with the present, then it can become harmful because it puts a greater amount of stress on the nervous system, circulatory system, our stress levels, and our minds.

over how you think about it, when you think about it, and if you think about it. You create more and clearer communication between your unconscious and conscious minds, allowing your morals, ethics, and integrity to match your behavior.

By the way, *just because you do not think about a memory does not mean you are disconnected from it.* We are able to bury memories or put them in a "box in a closet" and simply disassociate from them. These actions can leave us thinking that we have dealt with them and are no longer affected. Disassociation can be a dangerous coping strategy. If memories (events, emotions, people, etc.) are not dealt with, meaning healed, they will fester and come out, whether you like it or not. They can show up in your behavior, your mental abilities or condition, your physical abilities or condition, the quality of your relationships, and the quality of your life in general.

How do you know if you are disassociated or disconnected? Notice if you exhibit behaviors that you're not fond of and/or if you have to exert a great deal of mental power and will to not think about someone or not do something. If you can't explain it or don't really know why, you've probably allowed yourself to disassociate from the "cause." Here is another way to know, allow yourself to *really* think about the person, situation, or event you deem or deemed negative and become associated with it. When you truly sit with this memory for a while, how does it affect you? If it is hard to think about (is emotionally difficult), or you do not want to think about it or deal with it, you are probably disassociated. The memory is still there and has the wires running to it, but you are not allowing the experience to take place. This act is either due to fear or a lack of wanting to feel any type of pain or discomfort. Also, you may need to seek the guidance of a professional practitioner of NLP, hypnosis, PSYCH-K (applied kinesiology with belief statement work), or some other modality to help you associate and do any forgiveness work needed if there was a big trauma in your past. I suggest that any practitioners you work with should be thoroughly experienced and proficient in their modalities. I believe that any truly effective practitioner—this includes all doctors and nondoctors—has multiple certifications and/or licenses and is up to date on new studies and research in his or her field. OK, back to you and where you're at.

If you are experiencing less-than-beneficial emotions as you continue to think about a certain memory and are maybe thinking, "I did not realize I still felt this way," you were disassociated and are now becoming reassociated. Once you become reassociated with the memory, you have the opportunity to do the work that needs to be done to disconnect the difficult emotional wires attached to the memory. Once healing is truly accomplished, you can think about anything that may have been painful in the past and feel either calm, happy, love, or at peace with yourself. This is the sign that there are no more difficult emotional wires connected to the formerly nonbeneficial memory.

Remember what I said about the conscious and unconscious minds: the conscious mind is our goal-setter, and the unconscious mind is our goal-getter. If you are setting goals to do something or accomplish something and your behavior does not match your thoughts, ideas, and words, there is not a disconnect but either a lack of awareness or an awareness you have done nothing about. Both scenarios indicate disassociation. When we have an awareness around a memory, behavior, or emotion and do nothing to heal it, we are being irresponsible and placing our entire well-being at risk. Perhaps at the time when the awareness came to you, you did not know how to heal the memory, behavior, or emotion—and that is OK, but it is your job to then search for what *could* bring you the healing you need. You must associate with what ails you to "fix" it and heal. This does not mean you have to relive every gory detail, but it does mean that you acknowledge what it is you need to work on and go through the process (individually chosen) to heal.

Only by disconnecting from what ails you can you truly be more connected to what helps you to thrive, love, create, and live the life you imagine for yourself. Then, you become beneficially aligned, and your conscious and unconscious work in harmony for your greater good. You become better and better at communicating with yourself and others. This process also helps you to become more and more aware of the emotions tied to your memories and navigate what you need to either strengthen the beneficial connections or disconnect the nonbeneficial connections.

There is a big difference between dissociated and disconnected, and I hope I will make it very clear with the following metaphor and illustration.

DISASSOCIATED VERSUS DISCONNECTED

Even though the switches are in the off position, power is still being fed to the switches. At any time, the switches can be turned on and feed power to whatever they are wired to.

The switch is in the off position and also has no wires connected to it and no power feeding it; even if it were switched to the on position, no energy is present to activate it. It, the switch, simply is.

True forgiveness is breaking the emotional charge and energetic bond to our painful past, whatever that might be. What you're left with instead is a memory, and a memory without the emotional charge is called wisdom.
—Dr. Joe Dispenza

Forgiveness:

A Speech That Found Its Way into This Book

T he following is a speech I wrote and planned to deliver at a women's conference I was invited to speak at. Well, I decided not to speak at the event, for many reasons—no need to get into it. Simply, I chose to employ my boundaries. Although this speech has never be spoken to a group, it has been shared with my clients and friends. This speech is one of the most personal things I have ever shared with the public to date; that is changing. I wanted to add it to this book because, well, it is about forgiveness, but it also adds personal insight into me and my journey. I want to be as relatable as possible. I want to be transparent. I want to show up to serve those who have asked to be served. I hope that this speech allows you to see, feel, hear, and more deeply understand all that was previously written in this book. Enjoy.

We have many pursuits and only one journey. The journey lies within the pursuit. One such pursuit is forgiveness. I have a saying, "Unforgiveness is like plugging your ears when something smells really bad." I created this quote from a story a past teacher of mine told. The story goes like this: My teacher was teaching us a new technique within neuro-linguistic programming (NLP). The technique requires you to have had the experience of eating something terrible or having something in your mouth that tasted awful, something you would never want to eat again or really even come into contact with again. When he first learned this technique, it didn't really "land" because he hadn't experienced anything, to him, that was just plain gross. So he set out to find something that was not only disgusting but so disgusting that it was "fail-proof." He found *surstromming*. Apparently, there are some very interesting YouTube videos on this—watch at your own risk!

Surstromming is a fermented fish that put a shipping airplane out of commission because the cans exploded in transit, and they could never get the smell out. Anyway, my teacher procured a can of this fermented fish. Knowing the reputation of this fish, he felt it was best to open the can outside at a picnic table in the open air. His son, three years old at the time, was near him, as was his girlfriend. As soon as he popped open the can, the smell immediately started to permeate the air. His son started to cry, plugged his ears, shook his head vigorously back and forth, and said, "No, no, no . . . No, Daddy, make it stop! Make it go away! No, no, no, no." Years later, I was thinking about forgiveness and the vast misunderstanding of it, and this story came to my mind—what a great metaphor. I feel this story illustrates many people's understanding of forgiveness. Maybe you've heard it put this way, "Not forgiving is like drinking poison and expecting the other person to die."

If you still don't get what I mean, I'll spell it out a bit. The little boy plugged his ears to make the smell stop. That's not what makes smells go away. He needed to either plug his nose and pull his shirt up to breathe through his mouth or simply get the heck out of there!

When I talk about forgiveness with clients and various people, it seems that many people don't truly understand it. Many have a difficult time embracing it or utilizing it to its greatest depths of wholeness and healing. We humans tend to live in fear rather than LOVE, so we need forgiveness to get us out of these domains and remember LOVE. In LOVE, there is no longer anything left to let go of, and the word *forgiveness* even disappears. Forgiveness is simply being in a place of LOVE. LOVE is literally everything. It is void of judgment, void of discernment, void of separation, void of segregation, void of any separateness because it is a literally all-encompassing. And for some reason, this place of LOVE is not our default.

Fear and "not-love" are our default. Not-love is anger, sadness, hurt, grief, pain, loneliness, and so on. I reserve the not-love category for a small percentage of the population, dwelling in the not-love realm may be the only option—for example, psychopaths, sociopaths, and those individuals with a very low IQ and "temperament issues." The reason is that their brains are actually wired differently, and some parts are nonfunctioning. All they know is pleasure—pleasure void of fear and pleasure void of LOVE, just pleasure at all cost—because it's either pleasure or nothing. There is little concept, if any, of fear or even LOVE and the separation of the two. Now, fear is everything that is not-love, and it is all bigger and more amplified—there is more anger, segregation, separation, and division within fear. Fear is even more dangerous than not-love because fear is reactionary, and it is the fuel that intensifies anger, sadness, guilt, hurt, pain, grief, and loneliness. Fear takes us further away from LOVE and can sometimes make LOVE unrecognizable.

We have things in our society that perpetuate unforgiveness and fear; just one example is "#neverforget" or "forgive but never forget," which equals "#neverforgive" or "always remember." One of the biggest examples is 9/11. This is a very touchy and charged subject to this day. For the most part, we focus on the atrocities and the loss. We only came together for a short while and then disbanded—carrying around fear, anger, and grief and continuously projecting such feelings in our airports, places of business, religious houses, and individually. We are still focused on the pain and grief. What is gained from doing this? This only perpetuates segregation and more fear and allows the unhealthy cycle to continue and even grow. We must understand our fear to work through it. If we truly want to move past this, taking the lessons with us, we must find a way to come back together and create inclusivity.

All destruction comes with creation; it's built right in. Something dies or is destroyed, and then something else is created. Plant life is nourished by any creation that dies and decays, imparting nutrients into the soil it lies upon. We can embrace this idea in all its enormity, or we can—ignorantly and really stupidly—reject it. We can create more "move away from" or we can create more "move toward." Moving away from something only involves fear and all the subsets of emotions that come with it. Moving toward something involves LOVE. Moving toward something encourages hope. The destruction of segregation and fear will allow for the creation of inclusivity, community, healing, growth, and LOVE. When I talk to people about 9/11, shootings, and other traumas, I do not hear forgiveness in how they talk about such events or tell their stories. The pain is visceral and deep. I hear fear, a need for vindication, separation, and sadness. The sadness I hear is not for the simple fact that what happened is a sad occurrence but a sadness that is carried in every fiber of their being; it dredges up deep emotion—and very quickly. This is baggage; it is holding on to something and remembering what was, not what could be or any glimmer of anything learned. Although an event may be categorized as sad, we can still see the beauty that was created from it, such as a sense of community, the realization of bigger love, and the opportunity to learn more about a culture and ways we can work together to LOVE more and hate less. However, we seem to hold on to the hate and sadness, allowing the fear to segregate, separate, and continuously blame, cultivating the behavior of "moving away from" and not toward anything in particular. For the most part, we gather together in times of tragedy, but we fail to continue to work together to highlight, embrace, and enact the LOVE it takes to stay together outside of tragedy—the trauma fades for the moment, but it becomes even more greatly ignited when some future event occurs that sparks it. The embers were left unattended to continue to burn; the fire was never actually completely put out.

It seems hard to change our feelings and emotions about such tragic events because they seem to keep happening. One reason they keep happening is that we perpetuate the cycle of hate, which is based on fear. We live in fear, continuously feeling like we need to protect ourselves, separate ourselves, and steer clear of certain individuals, religions, and so forth. It would be healing if we allowed ourselves to gather together to learn about our differences—how to respect them, how to do our best to understand them—and even more importantly, to see how much more alike we are. We see differences when we are judging and justifying our own behavior against another's behavior. Our differences are, truly, so minute compared to all the similarities we share. Also, the minute and unique differences are what allow for change, growth, learning, invention, and evolution. To view ourselves or a certain religion, ethnicity, education, or community as better or holier is self-righteous, pompous, and elitist, as well as based on fear.

So I ask: What are you *always* remembering (never forgetting)? When you remember, are you remembering with an open heart? Are you remembering with gratitude, joy, love, or simple neutrality? Or are you remembering with sadness, guilt, rage, grief, or anything resembling these? Are you willing and/or able to see how your own hate, rage, anger, thoughts, comments, and so forth are no different from those that you are judging and comparing yourself to?

We make statements like, "They don't deserve forgiveness," or, even worse, "I don't deserve to be forgiven." First, who are you to judge that? Second, even if you think forgiveness is undeserved, please let that go and know that *you* deserve freedom. We want to be free from pain and grief, but we're "told" in so many ways to hold on to it. It makes us stronger. It makes us who we are. "What doesn't kill you makes you stronger." Although that statement holds truth, here's what's often left out: we must move *through* the difficult stuff to be free—to be the best version of ourselves. It's true that difficult experiences mold you into who you are, but if you hold on to them, you are a victim. You can only be strong for so long when carrying something around. If you heal through it, you gain the lessons—you are wiser and stronger for fully navigating the healing process, and you are lighter because there's nothing left to carry.

So why do we tend to protect that which we want to be free from? Why stay in pain—holding it in or carrying it around—when you could excuse it, learn from it, and heal through it? Why not just forgive?

Why not choose LOVE? When you're in a place of forgiveness, you've chosen to love yourself more than you hate someone or something else. Can you imagine what the world would be like if we all did this? I can! My imagination tells me it would be incredibly happier and healthier—with way less unnecessary suffering.

When you choose to forgive yourself, you create a space of possibility to experience LOVE, joy, happiness, and freedom in ways that are unimaginable when in a place of despair. When we forgive others, we forget the hate, anger, grief, and pain, not necessarily the event or person—although sometimes we do "forget" the person and event. When the grief and pain are no longer at the forefront, we allow other thoughts—happier and healthier thoughts—to take the now open space. It's not like our memories are wiped; it's just using a new filter to see through or a new program to operate from. If you really want to pull it up at some later point, you can, but it's no longer a difficult thing to think about, and there is no associated charge that zaps your mind, mood, or emotions.

Our ability to recall and repeat incessantly within our own minds is great and powerful. Natalie Fikes asks the "play button" question, and I've added to it. You may have done something you're less than proud of, or something may have happened to you without your permission, but who keeps pressing the play button? (You.) That play button is so hard to resist. It's right there; maybe there's even a big sign above it that tells you to leave alone or not to press it . . . Ohhh, but . . . it's also so irresistible. Some even become addicted to it; they are their own worst drug. They continuously see themselves as victims and set themselves up as victims—experiencing self-loathing, wanting, and needing and getting an unhealthy cortisol and dopamine rush every time the play button is pressed.

Victims rely on anyone, anything, everyone, and everything as their caregivers, to be their primary sources of energy and love, to be their uplifters, assurers, protectors, using them as their mental, emotional, spiritual, and even physical sources of sustenance and "energy food." Rarely, if ever, do they get these things from within or from things designed to restore their own energy. Rarely, if ever, do they go within to love, care for, and nurture themselves—they always need others. We must know that sometimes it's OK to rely on ourselves—it's actually imperative if you ever want to feel empowered. As long as you're a victim, someone or something else will always have control over you because you are giving that someone or something your permission.

As a victim, you will continue to tell your story, allowing the story to precede you. As a victim, you tell your story as though you are in it, not through it. Standing *in* your story is much different from standing *on* your story. As a victim, you abdicate your power; you subdue your courage; and you become disassociated from your soul, from your spirit, and from your light. When you completely rely on another, you deny *yourself*. You deny yourself the opportunity of great strength, wisdom, and deep LOVE. Yes, there is trauma. Yes, trauma can be difficult to decide to get through. I said *decide* on purpose.

It really is a decision to choose healing—to want to heal and learn from the trauma. Take from the trauma; don't let the trauma take you. There is a lesson in everything. The lesson could be as simple and profound as learning, realizing, and knowing just how strong you are; realizing how determined or tenacious you are; or being witness to your courageous ability to be bigger, happier, and healthier than what happened to you. The lesson could simply be to allow yourself to no longer reside in not-love or fear but to reside in LOVE.

A victim mentality is very different from a courageous mentality or what I call an "experiencer" mentality. A victim slinks and slouches; a victim stays on guard; a victim is reactionary; a victim creates and/or lives by excuses; a victim consistently relies on others and often feels shorted. Conversely, experiencers embrace and engage courage and bravery and come through to the other side—bringing with them lessons, knowledge, and most of all, wisdom. They take the knowledge, transform the experience into lessons, then evolve it and preserve as the knowledge deepens into wisdom.

The experiencer moves through life ready to experience more, ready to share, ready to show up, ready to continue healing and learning—ready for life itself. Experiencers take responsibility for themselves, understand the responsibility to themselves, and take responsibility for how they show up in their world and the world around them. They see themselves as stronger and more capable, not weaker, meeker, or incapable. The experiencer makes a decision to feel very differently about life and to actively live life free from past fear, past guilt, past anger, past pain, past hurt, and past grief. Experiencers decide that the past—whether a person, thing, and/or experience—no longer gets to control their thoughts, feelings, emotions, and other life experiences while they sit back and continually allow things to passively play out. The experiencer takes an active role in transforming his or her life. The experiencer never needs vindication.

The experiencer chooses freedom. The experiencer chooses joy and LOVE. The experiencer chooses to call the shots within his or her heart and mind. The experiencer receives nourishment from within. Experiencers rely on themselves and invite in help when and where needed, without feeling shorted, because there is no expectation on just how much help they "should" be getting from anyone else. They accept and appreciate any help and receive it all with gratitude.

You are the only one who can create your own freedom; no one can cage your spirit without your permission. So free your heart from the shackles, the wall, the cage. Grant yourself mercy. Your physical body can experience one thing while your heart, mind, soul, and spirit experience a completely different thing.

What's happening is merely happening; how you feel about it is another matter.

—*Neale Donald Walsch*

People ask me how I got here or what has happened to me that led me to this line of work. I have a litany of things I could list, but I'd have to spend some serious time remembering them all. See, I've done the work and continue to do the work. By doing the work, I have let go of the heavy, weighted emotions tied to and attached to people and events—without those ties and attachments, the memories float away. There's no need for them to be front of mind; there's no need for them to be so easily accessible. If I need the memory to relate, it'll come if it's meant to, and if it does, it simply flies in for the moment and flutters right away.

If I ever see that I'm allowing something from my past to dictate my present and possible future, I deal with it. I work through it. I'm no longer interested in carrying my bag of shit around, and I could care less about fancy-ass luggage. Also, I never compare pain or trauma. Everyone has a different threshold. Each culture, each family, each individual has a different threshold for grief, pain, and trauma. No one's trauma is bigger than anyone else's. What's easy for some to deal with would be nearly impossible for another to deal with, and vice versa.

Now, for the sake of relatability and transparency, here are just some of the things I've moved through. (By the way, I had to spend time remembering these.) My little list: bullied in elementary and middle school; molested at age ten; attempted suicide at age thirteen; my father living with multiple sclerosis from when I was twelve years old (1992) until he died on December 26, 2016; my mom going through breast cancer diagnosis and treatment in 2008–2009; times of caregiving and parenting both parents due to their health issues; having to close a successful business and walk away from a home that eventually went into foreclosure; bankruptcy; almost divorcing (twice); two different autoimmune illnesses; and some other stuff.

Each one of these things was a gift. They carved me into who I am today. I chose to learn from each of those things. I chose to heal from each of those things. I chose and still choose not to allow those things to define me, but to *be* the lessons I gleaned, live the lessons, experience deep gratitude, and actively turn what I learned into wisdom.

Some of my greatest teachers taught me exactly what I don't want to do, who I don't want to be, and how I definitely do not want to live. Their examples are invaluable—just as invaluable as the people who modeled for me how I want to live, think, be, and do. I allow myself to be the light for anyone who's up for seeing it and wants to know how to do the same for themselves.

Brené Brown said it wonderfully, "What's good about your pain is it's not my pain, and what's good about my pain is it's not your pain." Relating to pain is very different from experiencing it and/or carrying it, especially others' pain. Deal with your pain first and foremost, and then, only if you want, be witness to other people's pain. Never make their pain your pain—otherwise, the result is a boatload of people walking around "bleeding to death" together. That's not helpful, useful, or transformational. Let others have their pain, and allow them to work through it.

They have to acknowledge it, forgive it, and let it go all on their own—the only thing you can do is encourage them to do such a thing. Oh, and do this without being attached to the outcome. Attaching yourself to the outcome is attaching yourself to their pain—success or "failure" is all up to them. When you attach yourself to outcomes, you are often the one left wanting. You must stay in LOVE or risk residing in not-love and/or fear.

I chose and still choose forgiveness and mercy. Sometimes it doesn't feel easy, but I know what the alternative is, and I definitely am not interested in that. I'm interested in LOVE.

How do you know you're in a place of forgiveness? You see your past as an opportunity or gift. You think about your past with love and/or neutrality. It's about not allowing your past to dictate your future. It's about being a bit more in control of your emotions and knowing how to navigate them in a healthy way. We don't need our emotions controlling us and outweighing logic. There's that moment, just before you're going to lose your shit . . . or go down the hole of mental/emotional demise—that moment can be recognized or bypassed; it is a decision. It's so much healthier to recognize that moment so that you give yourself an opportunity to calibrate accordingly as much as possible. For some, it takes more work to get to or engage this "observer" role, and it's not a contest. It's about willingness, openness, determination, and patience. Forgiveness and mercy can change another person's life, and most of all, they can change your life, utterly and completely. LOVE really is the most powerful.

Here's a little synopsis of a story that shows grace, mercy, and forgiveness (maybe they're all the same.) Patton Oswalt is an actor and comedian. Randomly, a not-so-big-fan of his decided to verbally attack him on Twitter. Now, as I see it, he had a few options—ignore it, attack back, or show mercy and forgiveness; he opted for the third option. Patton decided to do a little digging on social media, and he found out that the guy had been going through a really rough time with his health and medical bills. The guy had created a GoFundMe page to try to raise money for himself, and Patton saw that he was far from his goal. Patton tweeted out to his followers to go to this guy's page and "deal him some good cards" because the ones he was dealing with at that moment were "shitty."

Within twenty-four hours, over $35,000 was raised for this guy by people deciding to show more LOVE rather than fighting back with hate. This man's goal was exceeded by more than five times his original goal. When the man saw this, he responded with a tweet back to Patton explaining how humbled and sorry he was. He said he had a family member in need as well, and he was going to pay it forward. He realized how harmful his words were and could not compose enough words to describe the gratitude he was experiencing.

Even though this random guy put out hate, he received LOVE in return, and it transformed his life. Patton's Twitter followers were presented with a leader who chose to lead by example, and he gave each of them not only permission to rise above but also the opportunity to be leaders themselves.

Imagine what could happen if we all put our precious egos aside and were able to rise above hate with LOVE, no matter what. How would this world transform? That is a world I want to reside in. You can choose, now, for that to be the world you reside in as well.

Forgiveness:

Grace and Mercy

G race happens when the ego is tamed, nourished, and healthy (as opposed to a mal-
nourished, deprived, out-of-control ego).
Grace is strength, vulnerability, and unyielding
LOVE. It is the feeling and action of choosing peace
over the insatiable need to be right or "better than."
Grace is a gift of the heart from the heart.

Mercy is very similar to grace in that it includes
everything I defined about grace, then radically in-
corporates magnanimous LOVE. Mercy is *you* putting out the fire *another* set in an attempt to harm,
maim, or even kill you—all while encouraging others
to join you in delivering kindness and LOVE to the
"transgressor."

Forgiveness needs grace and mercy. This means
letting go of harsh judgments, refraining from "point-
ing the finger" and shaming. We're all too quick to

hold someone else to the fire. We don't like it when it's done to us, but that's not what's going on in our minds when we do it to another. Social media has made it easy to have anonymity while spewing and spurring hate, shame, judgment, and anger. Many times, this is just a projection of our own guilt, anger, fear, and so forth—none of which is an excuse to place our own shit on another. It's time we take responsibility for ourselves and make better efforts.

Most of the time, we don't even know the whole story, but—damn—we are quick to "snapshot" this one thing, more than likely taken out of context, and then fire at will until out of ammo. Most of what we see and read is a small part of the bigger picture. Many things are taken out of context, and then the content is reframed to fit the skewed message it is intended to deliver. We seem to need to bring ourselves up by comparing and justifying: "I'm not as bad as so and so"; "At least I didn't do x, y, z"; "The candidate I love has only done three bad things—that's not as bad as the five things your candidate has done, I think your candidate's way worse."

Grace and mercy start with you. What do you want to put out there? How do you want to feel? What do you want to experience more of? Your actions determine this. Your words determine this. Your beliefs determine this. Follow the moral compass of *your own* heart.

Not one of us is perfect. Not one of us is without some sort of baggage. It is our responsibility to deal with our stuff. The healthier you are, the healthier the world around you becomes. Leading by example does not mean you are better; it means you are more aware, and it means you are willing to take a second and third look at people and situations, as well as yourself, to gain as much information as possible before making a decision on how you *really* feel. Before forming an opinion, ask yourself, "Is this the whole picture? Is this possibly one person's opinion formed from skewed information?" Being responsible to and for yourself also means you are willing to change your mind as you learn more. It means you are willing to be wrong and evolve with new information.

Grace and mercy are a responsibility. You are responsible for giving yourself grace and mercy first. Showing grace and mercy is good for your soul, good for healing, and good for connecting. Instead of skewering someone else for a bad day, a lapse in judgment, or a lack of patience, remember moments, even months or years, that were difficult for you. You have had times where your behavior and/or words were not shining in their best light. Allow your mind to soften, your emotions to calm, and think of some way, any way, you could relate. This brings peace to your heart and helps to remove the possibility of spreading and encouraging more hate and abuse in the world.

Grace and mercy are imperative to forgiveness. It's all about "softening the heart." There is no need to fight anger with anger, fear with fear, or hurt with unkind words and actions. Forgiveness is never about fighting, battling, or struggling. Grace and mercy are what help transform "the fight" into a peaceful, awakened movement. Practice grace and mercy—you will find your way to total forgiveness and create a movement in your life and the lives around you.

You must give grace and mercy with steadfast boundaries. You encourage LOVE and healing, and you keep distance when needed. No relationship of any kind is required. Giving grace and mercy and accomplishing forgiveness in no way sanction the continuation of toxic interactions or relationships.

You can take necessary steps and enforce necessary processes, all while giving grace and mercy and accomplishing forgiveness. You do what is required for safety and needed to continue in the realm of LOVE. You do what you need to do with LOVE.

Forgiveness:

It's More Than Nice; It's Kind

Forgiveness feels nice, but more importantly, it is kind. Forgiveness is always a kindness you do for yourself and others. Many people engage in what may appear to be nice behaviors, but they are actually detrimental and unkind. Examples of detrimental behaviors include holding a grudge, engaging in a relationship or activity out of obligation (not commitment), not allowing people to get to know you or only letting certain people "in," and eating food you don't like or are sensitive/allergic to just because someone made it for you. Some of those may seem "nice," but they are all unkind, inauthentic, and enabling. None are congruent, aligned, authentic, or honest. Kind is always nice, but nice is not always kind. Kind is always honest; nice can be dishonest.

Sure, it's nice to be nice, but nice can "turn a blind eye." Nice doesn't rock the boat, nice doesn't create tension, nice doesn't necessarily tell the truth, nice can be misleading, nice can be avoiding, and nice can be downright detrimental and cruel. The more you are only nice and the less you are kind, the more you teach yourself to be inauthentic and also teach those around you that it's OK to be inauthentic within the relationship. You teach everyone you meet how to love you, like you, and treat you by what you allow and how you show up in each situation and relationship. Kindness, however, has an authentic truth built into it, although sometimes truth doesn't seem nice in the moment.

If you never face hardships, you grow very little. Kindness allows room for growth that moments of nice never will. Kindness is sometimes having uncomfortable conversations. Kindness is sometimes putting space in a relationship. Kindness sometimes means not "helping" a person at all. Kindness requires you to dig deep, go with your heart, engage integrity, listen to your soul, and steadfastly enact the words and behavior that exemplify truth and LOVE.

Here are some examples to show you what I mean by all of this:

Example 1: One of my dogs loves to ride in my lap while I'm driving. In fact, he will whine and shake if he does not get to do this, which is upsetting to him and me. So I give in and allow him to ride on my lap—it pacifies both of us. I have let him do this for so long that to create a healthy separation with a safe space in back and him not being with me would seem unkind to him and not nice, but that is not the truth. It feels good to have him close and to be traveling around with my fur baby on my lap. Both of us enjoy the "snuggle time," and neither of us is upset or stressed. He's got me trained well!

Here's the thing. This is nice, but it's unkind. If I were to get into an accident, he would be the first one hurt, possibly even killed (due to the proximity of the airbag). I would feel awful and have to do a lot of work to forgive myself for not doing what I know is better and ultimately "right" and kind.

Really, I'm enabling him, and he is enabling me. I'm being nice by letting him ride in my lap. I'm telling him it's OK to manipulate me with his whining and poor behavior when he doesn't get his way. I am not doing myself or him a kindness by allowing him on my lap and not getting a screen and a comfy bed for the back so that he is safe and has a way to be as comfortable as possible.

Example 2: A family was sitting around a table, eating and chatting. There were a few different conversations going on. A couple of the members started to talk politics, and then it went beyond politics to ethnicity. The things being said were mean, very opinionated (void of real truth, fact, or even statistics), fear based, and backed with anger, and they placed blame.

A third party was in on the conversation until it got to that point and then "tapped out" because this person felt disheartened and disappointed by the family members having the conversation and didn't have anything agreeable to contribute to the discussion. Instead of offering counterpoints or letting them know that what was being said was racist, bigoted, and just plain cruel, this person turned to engage in a different conversation at the table—leaving that other conversation to be continued—all the while feeling a bit guilty for not saying anything and even more uncomfortable and sad about what was being said. It felt "nicer" to just leave it alone and not upset the family gathering. Instead, the person pivoted and engaged in a nice conversation about a kid who did something thoughtful for his parents.

The person was being "nice" just to leave the conversation and engage in a more uplifting conversation. In this case, nice, inadvertently, promoted racism and taught the people involved in the conversation that it's OK to continue such a conversation—even around a person who is deeply affected by it—and that no different behaviors or thought processes are appreciated, required, or encouraged. The cycle is left to perpetuate.

This person regretted not saying anything and felt guilty for not using their voice. The person felt as though, in that situation, they were a contributor to the problem instead of a voice for a possible solution. Self-forgiveness was a must in this situation; so was forgiving the other parties involved. It could not be changed after the fact, but moving forward, thoughts, feelings, and behaviors could change so long as resentment was let go.

This person realized that in the future, they may not be able to say anything in the moment, but that doesn't mean that nothing could ever be said. They realized the family members could be invited out or over for a one-on-one conversation or write a letter or email to express personal emotions in a kind and loving way, sharing ideas that could possibly offer the other parties some new "food for thought."

It is unkind to yourself not to defend your heart when something affects it deeply. It is also unkind not to defend or uphold a bigger idea of LOVE, inclusion, community, and kindness toward other beings. In this case, kindness would have meant being extremely uncomfortable and challenging the status quo. It also would have been authentic and in alignment with respecting and honoring this person's heart and the hearts of those unknowingly being accused.

Example 3: A kid continuously forgets to bring something that they need to school, leaving it at home. The parent, feeling sorry for the kid and wanting to go above and beyond all the time to help, leaves work or other tasks to go home, get the thing the kid needs, and bring it to school. This happens almost daily. The kid is reminded by others to remember what is needed, but disregards the reminders because the parent continuously enables the kid. The kid knows how manipulate and rely on the parent no matter what, so there's no need to learn to remember or plan. (Side note, the kid in the story is not dealing with mental or physical limitations.)

Although this is nice to do for the kid, it's ultimately detrimental and unkind. The parent is teaching the kid to be reliant on the parent, instead of the kid being able to rely on self-independence. The parent is possibly jeopardizing her job or some relationship by prioritizing the child's forgetfulness and/or irresponsibleness. The kid is not learning how to take responsibility for individual needs, how to prioritize, or how to think ahead and plan.

When people don't learn how to rely on themselves and constantly rely on others, they live a debilitating, disempowered, limited life. They often feel like a victim, feel entitled, and are frustrated when fumbling through the tough navigation of life. When something doesn't go right, they are not equipped with the skills to troubleshoot, problem solve, and know that they have what it takes to get through the situation at hand.

When we know better, it's our responsibility to do better. Another person may not understand why we are doing something and feel deeply hurt, distraught, or angry over it, but all we can do is do our best to explain why we are doing whatever we're doing. Others may or may not understand; that is not our concern, worry, or responsibility; so long as we are doing something out of love and kindness, we are doing our best.

Forgive what you don't understand, forgive yourself for not understanding it, and forgive others for seeming to not understand. Speak the truth of your heart with kindness and love. Kindness is direct; niceness can be passive-aggressive or just plain passive. Kindness speaks in words and actions when needed most, whereas niceness can stay silent or still. Kindness is void of anger and blame. Kindness allows you to take responsibility for yourself and have a responsibility to yourself. Kindness allows space for learning, healing, and growing. When you experience the occasional difficulty in being kind to others, do yourself a kindness and practice forgiveness—know in your heart and mind that by being kind, you exercised your best.

It's nice to hold the door for someone, smile at another, say hello, pay a compliment, or put a shopping cart away that's not yours. There are times and places for being nice, so be nice when it's called for, and always be kind.

Practicing kindness creates more possibilities for forgiveness because it already leads the way with LOVE. Forgiveness is a kindness you bestow on your own heart.

Forgiveness:

For You to Cultivate

Whoen you think of forgiveness, think about pardoning and excusing the limitations that happen to be present in your life, however they show up. It is up to each one of us to forgive the limitations and negativity from within us. It does not matter what anybody else did because we cannot control another person—we can only control ourselves. It is up to you to create the freedom you desire in your life by employing forgiveness at such a deep level that anytime something happens, you only take in the lessons and learnings. Decipher the lessons, and then choose to fully forgive anything negative that resides within your being. Then, you can move forward positively for the sake of yourself and the sake of your future.

Not everything is in your control, but your filters, beliefs, and behaviors are. They provide the perception of our reality. This is how we get to decide how we feel about something or toward someone, including ourselves. We get to decide which switches are powered by the main breaker and which ones no longer have wires running to them. Keep that in mind when you look at some of the remarkable people who have done some amazing things in our world. Maya Angelou and Nelson Mandela are just two examples. The things they went through, by most accounts, were horrific, yet they were able to employ forgiveness fully. They chose to create happiness, success, and purpose in their lives. Forgiveness is the only reason they were able to move forward and be as incredible as they were able to be. If they were unwilling to embrace forgiveness, they would forever have seen themselves as the victim. They would forever have had something to complain about, fall back on, limit themselves, keeping them from being who they were and the preventing the extraordinary impacts they had on their own lives as well as the world.

When practicing forgiveness, remember to forgive often and forgive fully. Be conscientious regarding what you are practicing. I heard this saying from one of my past teachers: "Practice does not make perfect; practice makes permanent." There is a lot of truth to this. It could also be said that practice does make perfect, but perfectly good or perfectly awful. Here is an example of what I mean: If you are practicing a language and you learn a new word, you practice saying it over and over. If you continue to pronounce a word incorrectly, which you assumed was correct when you started, and then learn the word is different from what you were saying, how long before you are able to successfully and consistently say the word correctly? Then, how much or how hard do you have to think about the *correct word* each time before saying it? Another example is learning and practicing a golf swing. It can be really hard to train our bodies to move one way, only to find out that we need to move a completely different way. Man, golf is frustrating, even for the pros, who seem to have golf coaches changing their swings every so often and thus changing their game. (See what I did there. *Wink.*)

Make sure that what you are practicing is creating the result you are aiming for, and if it is not, tweak it so that you achieve your desired results. Choose to be responsible, choose to employ forgiveness, and have fun *creating your life*!

Forgiveness:

Questions and "Answers"

I asked people on Facebook to message me with questions they had about forgiveness. This was my opportunity to see what information people really wanted. Here are the questions that I answered and thought important to include.

Is forgiveness easy?

Yes and no. The concept can be easy and the process simple (not necessarily easy), but the actuality of being in a place of forgiveness is not always easy. You do not forgive because someone has asked for it; in fact, you forgive regardless of whether someone has asked for it or not. You forgive regardless of whether you think it's deserved or not. If you feel the other is undeserving, you are in a place of judgment and setting yourself up to harness detrimental feelings. If you think you are undeserving, you are setting yourself up to experience harmful repercussions. Remember, forgiveness is always for you, not the other person. Once forgiveness is accomplished, it has the opportunity to benefit the other, but that is not the goal. You have to be ready, able, and willing in order to forgive: *ready* to forgive and let go of negativity, *able* to go through the process (as many times as needed), and *willing* to live life in a different state of being after empowering forgiveness within it. Sometimes, going through the process of forgiveness needs to be done more than once to really feel free from the person, situation, or thing. Your emotional tie to that thing, person, situation, or a combination of them determines how easy and long the process will be.

Is forgiveness just for people?

No. We tend to have relationships with things, entire situations, animals, money, food, and so forth. I have worked with people and helped them through the process of forgiving with things like jobs, money, homes, cars, an animal that bit or attacked them earlier in life, and many others. Anything you think of that makes you cringe, sad, mad, or unhappy in any way can be forgiven. Everything is energy. The amount and type of energy we have toward or about something determines its worth to us. The worth of something determines how it affects us, and how it affects us is how we can decipher whether or not the energy is good or bad. When we become aware of something's unsettling or nonbeneficial energy, we get to determine if forgiveness is needed and appropriate.

How do I begin the process of forgiveness, or where do I start?

Think about the person(s), situation(s), or thing(s) that seem to have a negative charge around them. This can be family, friends, coworkers, a stranger, your job, money, food, excess weight, religion, yourself, and so on. Understand *what* it is you need to forgive. Once you have a clear understanding/knowing about this, you can begin to have the conversation between you and it or them within your mind (or aloud), which leads to freeing yourself of the unresolved thoughts and emotions. The point is to reframe, resolve, shed, and remove these negative charges and, instead, feel calm, happy, content, peaceful, optimistic, loving, joyful, creative, and more positive in your understanding/realization/outlook.

How do you reframe or empathize? Empathizing is very different from sympathizing. To sympathize is to "feel sorry for." Forgiveness is never about feeling sorry for anyone. As soon as you feel sorry for someone, you categorize that person as a victim. Empathizing is about acknowledging what someone has gone through or is going through and respecting the situation for what it is. When empathizing, there are times when you will be able to identify with people and what they have gone through, and there will be times where you will not, but you feel the depth of what they are describing.

Sometimes, it helps to reframe and think of the person you want to forgive as a wounded child—after all, the unresolved emotion and behavior usually stem from childhood experiences. Try to analyze the person, thing, or situation in relation to the fact that you also had horrible or less-than-perfect experiences growing up or at some point in life. What if the other person had experiences you have only thought about and about which you came to the conclusion, "I could never handle *that*," yet the other person actually went through it?

We tend to behave in a way that was or is conducive to our environment. Often, people are just treating us the way they were treated. How sad is that to think about? (Let the sadness be only a momentary agent that helps you flip how you internalize the person.) This is what helps me change my point of view. I let go of what I think I know or how it "should" be, then let go of the difficult emotions and negative charge around the memories. I get to choose to be in a frame of mind that only benefits *me*. I remind myself that this person may not know any better or may have had it worse than I did. This is not an excuse for their behavior but an excusing of the negative charge I have tied to their lack of awareness. Also, there is always the slim possibility that this person is incapable of love, for there are people with *severe* mental issues who are incapable of love. (To be walked through the process of forgiveness that I learned, visit www.thepursuitofforgiveness.com to purchase the recordings.)

Do I have to forgive to properly heal?

Yes. If you have ever felt wronged or like you did wrong, you must forgive to heal. To me, being in a place of forgiveness means peace, calm, freedom, and LOVE. I do not believe you have to love the one who you feel wronged you; you simply need to feel at peace with him or her or the situation and not feel any need for revenge or any feelings of anger or the like. You can be in a place of, let us call it, *Zen*, where you no longer *care*. Either way, you're happy and content. Let me further define what I mean by "lack of care." I mean that there is a feeling of *nothingness*, with no void. You do not wish for harm but, rather, for the best, whether you continue the relationship or wish it from afar.

If you can think about a person or situation from your past (I mean really think) and feel Zen about it all, you have probably done the work. If you have any difficult feelings or negatively-charged thoughts that come up, there may still be some work to do. Anytime we harbor negativity in our bodies, there is always a possibility of it manifesting into something we may find less than desirable. Whether it be a behavior, illness, or limiting belief, if we do not deal with our negativity properly, it will find a way to deal with itself. This is why we need things like forgiveness processes, therapists, neuro-linguistic programming (NLP), hypnotherapy, PSYCH-K, and other modalities of healing. Forgiveness is the most important first step, and sometimes, it can be enough for it to be the only one.

Am I in need of forgiveness?

Yes, we are usually hardest on ourselves. Do you feel like you have ever done anything wrong? How are your self-talk and self-image? If those things are anything less than wonderful, take some time to find out what it is within you that requires care, attention, love, and reconciliation, and take time to forgive and let those things go for the sake of your all-around health and well-being. After all, as I've mentioned on a few occasions, forgiveness is ultimately for you; the secondary benefits are just bonuses.

What does it mean to forgive if forgiving means we have to let go of or take time away from people or things?

To forgive is to take responsibility for yourself, to create change for the better, whatever that means for you, and to live a life experiencing more LOVE, calm, and freedom. Sometimes, we cannot see what it is in our lives that is not serving our greatest potential or highest good. Many times, there is simply not an awareness around this thing, or we are in denial and unwilling to deal with it. Not every person or thing in our lives is good for us, but we, as humans, tend to have a hard time letting go, even if we know that we need to let go for the sake of ourselves.

Consider people who smoke, drink too much, do drugs, eat too much, eat unhealthy food, or stay in abusive relationships. Many are aware of what they are doing, yet they continue to do it. Some continue because they do not know how to change things, some prefer denial, some are scared, some feel trapped, and others simply do not care enough about themselves or the people around them. We are not meant to hold on to everything and everyone in life.

There is that saying, paraphrased, that people may come into your life for a minute, an hour, a month, years, or a lifetime. Each person is there because you are either a lesson for him or her or he or she is a lesson for you. The people who teach us continuously tend to be the ones we keep around the longest, and we are usually around those people more often. This is not to say they are the healthiest of relationships, but they can be. Some people, however, keep the unhealthiest relationships around. They do the same things over and over without integrating the lessons and learnings and are unable to move on or move forward without the unhealthy connection.

This scenario is where forgiveness can start the process of eliminating the unhealthy relationships and allowing you to be OK with the elimination.

How do I know if I'm really in a place of forgiveness?

When you can think about the person, thing, or situation and not feel sadness, anger, dismay, stress, frustration, or any other negatively-charged thought, feeling, or emotion, you are *probably*[3] there. Also, if you are in a place of only wishing good or positive things for that person, thing, or situation, you are *probably* there. If the person, thing, or situation comes into your mind and goes right back out without a "charge," you are *probably* there. You can ask yourself, "Am I in a place of forgiveness about _____?" If the very first answer of your inner voice says yes, you are *probably* there. There is nothing negative about being in a continual state of forgiveness.

Do I continually have to forgive?

Yes and no. There is that saying, "Forgive fully and forgive often." Forgiveness is a choice and something

---

3 I say *probably* because only you can truly know these answers for yourself.

that seems to be a constant in life. If you have forgiven a person, thing, or situation that you will likely never come across again (but would not care if you did) and feel you are really in a place of forgiveness, you're probably done. If you have forgiven a person, thing, or situation and really feel good toward him or her or it, but then something else happens that changes that feeling, then, yes, you will probably need to go through the process again. It is always beneficial to be in a place of forgiveness. If you are unsure whether you are there, go through the process again; it will only help.

Is it necessary?

Yes. Forgive all that will help you move through your life while being happier, healthier, and more often in LOVE. Also, not everything needs a forgiveness process. If you are walking around your house and simply stub your toe on accident, you most likely will be able to let that go pretty quickly and be fine. Now, if you stub your toe and immediately say something like, "damn it, so-and-so," then you might need to look at what needs to be forgiven with *so-and-so*, as well as with yourself. When something small brings up big feelings, it means there is something unresolved (either currently or in the past). As another example, say you drop your favorite mug that was given to you by someone or belonged to someone you love, and it breaks. If you feel heartbroken or any degree of sadness and that feeling does not leave for an extended period, such as more than a day, there might be some self-forgiveness to be done. Also, if you are finding yourself mourning after the event, you will definitely need to do self-forgiveness and may want to look into doing more healing work—not necessarily around the event but around you and the person or situation that has to do with the mug.

How do I forgive someone who continues to hurt/harm me?

Forgiveness is about releasing pain from within you. It is not about excusing the other person's behavior. You can accept the person, if you choose, and not accept the behavior. Remember, you can only change your behavior and your perception of the situation and the world around you, and only you can change the way you feel about something. You absolutely cannot change any of those things within another being. Forgiving and releasing do not mean you have to continue any sort of relationship with the person, thing, or situation. If the toxicity is detrimental and the other person is not willing to also go through the forgiveness process, you have to decide what it is you are willing to accept. If you do move forward in the relationship, what other boundaries need to be established? How many times will you allow the boundaries to be bulldozed? Continue to forgive yourself and the other person, as well. If healing, well-being, happiness, and a sense of love within you are not achieved, it may be a good idea to remove yourself from the relationship with this person, thing, or situation. If you need to, you can always love from afar.

How do I forgive and let go as a parent?

This is probably one of the hardest things to do for many, and it is one I have seen successfully done. You get to decide how much you can take, of anything, in life. Again, we cannot change anyone, not even our own children. I have seen parents who have needed to forgive and completely let go of their kids because of the possible harm to their lives. If these parents had not taken this step, they would be the ones in prison or jail or getting sued for thousands or millions of dollars. Yes, these are extreme, and probably the most hurtful, examples. If these parents are able to say, "I love you, but I will not allow you to ruin my life along with yours," they are setting the boundaries needed with their children, which I think anyone is capable of. Some need to be loved for a short time or from afar, some need lots of time with the space, and some experience forgiveness with no hope for a future relationship. These are situations where forgiveness work probably needs to be done on at least a daily basis, in conjunction with other healing modalities, until you feel some sort of wonderful shift.

How do I forgive my parents?

Well, first remove them from the pedestal you placed them on. Remove superhero expectations of them. Then, look at yourself. Are you perfect? Are you trying your best and working diligently to navigate this "life thing"? Do you have kids? Do your kids love everything you do? Have you done things that you regret (as a parent or otherwise)? The truthful reality is that not everyone is cut out to be a parent, let alone a good one. The circumstances of life get in *everyone's* way. Just because you are responsible for a little life doesn't mean you understand the responsibility, uphold the responsibility, or even navigate the responsibility well. We are each our own soul, with unique quirks, personalities, beliefs, characteristics, behaviors, and so forth.

You are probably doing your best, and I'm going to venture to guess that your parents were attempting to do their best (if they even understood what their best was/is). Your parents' behavior and presence (or lack thereof) stem from belief systems. These belief systems may have been formed by their family members, community, church, school, friends, things that they experienced, a lack of self-worth, and so on. It's time to look at your parents as just other fellow human beings navigating this messy, crazy, silly, beautiful, confusing world. Their misbehavior, abuse, absence, or other transgression happened—it cannot be taken back. The only way to go is forward.

You can go forward holding a grudge; exhaust yourself by trying to hold them to the fire; and/or deplete yourself by carrying bags of anger, hurt, grief, and other difficult emotions—these are options. The other option is to realize that by doing this, you are still giving them control over your mental, emotional, physical, and even spiritual health and well-being. Do your best to look through a lens of compassion for anything they might have dealt with in their lives.

This is not offering excuses or excusing behaviors; it's merely offering yourself a different point of view for the sake of bringing peace to *your* heart.

Allow yourself to see them as a teacher. They taught you exactly what you do and do not want in your life. They taught you how you do and do not want to be treated. They taught you how you do and do not want to live your life. If you are living the same life or a worse life than they did and are feeling pissed about it, you are still allowing them to make the decisions for you and your life. You are allowing the "ghost" of them to echo in your heart and mind. They are essentially living rent-free within your being. Your being is not for rent, and the only one who should be dwelling deep within is *your* soul—equipped with a megaphone that only speaks the truth of *your* heart. Kick any tenants out; take back the keys; remove the lock; and cut the cords of pain, grief, anger, and so forth. Free yourself by letting the past go and redeciding how you want to *live your life*.

You have to stop being their victim; you have to stop being a victim in your own mind. Free yourself from victimhood and *experience* the life that *you* want. Be stronger, happier, and more loving than the pain of the past—you are capable of this; now remind yourself of this. No one can remove your inner strength but you. Being idle or consistently carrying too much weight is the only way to become weaker, and you can do something about both of those things—if you choose.

You are the keeper of your heart and mind; you are the one who opens the door to allow in what you want and need. Be the decision maker in your life. Decide who and what will stay in your life and who and what will go—do this in accordance with *your* heart, not by the direction of *anyone else*. Decide who and what you keep company with and who and what you avoid. *Toxic is toxic*—recognize it, and remove it from your life. If the toxic person or thing transforms and you feel it could now provide nourishment, healing, and goodness, then invite it back in—but only if you want to.

Why is forgiveness so hard?

Forgiveness is a process, one that can be either short or very long. You have to be ready, willing, and able to give up your excuses, reasons, and that little ego voice—you have to truly want things to be *better* in your life. For you to know what better is requires the process to be done. Better is sometimes hard to get to, but if you are trying to achieve it, it is worth the time and effort. For many, change is a difficult thing because it often means giving up what is familiar; although what is familiar may be undesirable, it is what we know. The unknown can be scary, and because it is the unknown, we cannot be sure it is going to be better.

Often, we opt not to do the work it takes to delve into the unknown and deal with the discomfort that change can sometimes bring. Discomfort is what you make of it, and really, nothing is a guarantee, but if your truth and purpose are strong within, then be willing to bet on yourself. Not all individuals have faith in themselves and their abilities. This is one reason I encourage people to do self-forgiveness first, and on a daily basis, until they feel a wonderful shift.

When we are strong within ourselves, it is easier to forgive others. When we are strong within ourselves, we are more likely to rely on ourselves for the care, love, compassion, and changes we need to make in life. We become responsible to ourselves, and when we take on that responsibility, we get to decide how we want to handle the possible discomfort and navigate it in a way that brings about the most powerfully positive outcome.

Sometimes you have to sit with the discomfort and the pain. Sometimes you have to understand why it's there, why you held on to it, and what its message is. All pain has a message; you have to be willing to hear it. Also, sometimes the message is small and simple, not at all the enormity we conjured it up to be. Allow yourself to engage with the discomfort and pain as if they were a little child with an important message; this can help with it not seeming so gnarly, big, and scary. Then, work with that little child delivering the message to you. Show gratitude for the delivering of the message and for receiving the message.

Healing can be hard and difficult work, but the payout of getting through your problems is so, so very sweet—you'll wonder why you waited so long. Once you get a taste of freedom, you'll never want to allow your problems to capture, enslave, or hold you down ever again.

What if the other person refuses to forgive me or someone I love?

If people refuse to forgive, there is nothing you can do about that. That is a burden the other must deal with. The best thing you can do is forgive yourself and forgive those people. They may live with no forgiveness in their hearts, minds, bodies, and lives, but you do not need to do the same.

Remember, we are not meant to have a relationship with every single person in this world. Whether we had a great relationship with someone in the past or believe that we can have a great relationship with that person in the future, there will be no future relationship if he or she is unwilling to forgive. You can move past that. When others choose not to forgive, they will be the ones who have to live with it. You will experience peace and healing if you forgive yourself and the other person. The forgiveness you create and allow in your life grants you the opportunity to move forward positively, with or without someone or something.

Why can God forgive me for anything I have done, yet forgiving myself is one of my greatest challenges?

Every person I have met has a different idea of *God* and what God entails. I'm going to answer this question using the word *God* because that is how it was asked, but if you use a different word, such as

Universe, Spirit, Holy Spirit, The Matrix, Divine, Energy, Holy Light, higher self, LOVE, Life Source, Life Force or anything else, please insert *your* word in place of *God.*

If God is part of us, then we are part of God. To put it another way, God is not outside of us but within us. Being that God is forgiving, what is holding you back from forgiving yourself? What about you is so unforgivable? We are the only ones who can limit us, and this limitation is not what is intended by God. We are meant to co-create our lives with God, not pray and sit back so that it can all happen and unfold in front of us without lifting a finger. You don't pray or meditate to manifest your goals and then sit back on the couch to watch TV or scroll social media. We must engage in the prayer and the action that follows that prayer. If we are really using the gift that resides within us, we are empowering that powerful part of us that knows how to forgive. This empowerment is the part of us that gets us through the process and helps us make decisions out of love for ourselves. We can trust that even in dark times or moments, we are learning, gaining lessons, and creating a strong foundation to build our lives on. As our faith in God grows, so should our faith in ourselves; it is a symbiotic relationship—as much as we respect God, we respect ourselves.

If you found out you were going to die tomorrow, which people or things would you need to forgive?

This is your opportunity to answer this question for your life, and the answer could be anyone, including *yourself.*

Forgiveness:

Move Your Life Forward

It really is impossible to move forward while holding on to the illusion of what the past serves. Holding on to the past creates the excuses you need to keep you from moving forward.

Instead of being angry that another person was "able to move on so easily," do the same—let go, move on, and free yourself. That person already has, and if that is not true, it is not your issue.

Sometimes people hold on to pain to make themselves right—a self-fulfilling prophecy. They justify how they feel and behave due to how they were treated at some point in the past. How do you make yourself right? (In the following examples, I am using the word *you* in a general sense for ease of reading.) One example is thinking and believing, "She is just going to leave me like all the rest," then behaving in ways that push the person away. She finally can't deal with your behavior anymore and leaves. You then think poorly of her and maybe even yourself, thus making you "right" in your belief. Another example is you believing that another person thinks or feels something that was never clarified, such as, "He thinks he's better than me." (Really, you are the one who thinks he is better than you.) Maybe that other person completes something with ease or accomplishes what you wanted to accomplish. Then, he either offers to help you with completing the same thing or emphatically shares his accomplishment with you. You are not where he is, and it's because, in this competition that *you* created, your frustration got in the way of doing what you needed to focus on—you may have also allowed your lack of self-worth to take the wheel. You respond to this person's offer of help or enthusiasm in a less-than-ideal way by saying something to the effect of, "You don't think I can do this myself?" Or a short, snide, "Good for you."

In making yourself right, you exhibit behaviors and emotions based on beliefs that perpetuate self-fulfilling prophecies and also look like self-sabotage. The outcome of the behavior tends to appear as if it was the other person the whole time because it turned out exactly as you thought it would. Any feelings of being less than, not good enough, or un-lovable are not true and can be changed when you realize that you operate from those beliefs. Holding such beliefs has a tendency to cause us to project these insecure emotions onto another person, and then we assume that person thinks or feels a certain way about us that has never been confirmed by actually asking the other person.

Negative patterns tend to repeat until completely dealt with. People holding on to pain make themselves right—but at a cost. Illness follows. Physical, mental, and emotional illnesses are conceived under the stress of continuing to hold on to painful feelings and limiting beliefs. Those, if nothing else, are the greatest reasons to forgive. Forgive fully, and the pain leaves. Forgive fully, and you get to be the one who experiences triumph. *Triumph is in the forgiveness.*

Forgiveness:

"Mantra"

Sometimes it can be hard to think about forgiving someone, especially yourself. It may be difficult to get into a space and place where you feel ready, and sometimes, it is hard to know where to start. Taking anything one day at a time makes anything feasible and anything you want to accomplish possible (except actually sprouting wings and flying as a human being, but you can create the image and feeling). Give yourself permission to start somewhere!

With the following mantra, I am providing you with something you can repeat every morning before you start your day or every evening before you go to bed. You may even repeat this multiple times during the day. The more you use it, the more you create a readiness to forgive, the more you create a space to implement freedom, and the more you keep the lens through which you look at life clean and clear.

If you want to just read the first paragraph and work your way into the second paragraph, wonderful. If you want to read the whole thing, wonderful. Do what you are inclined to, as you are able, and challenge yourself to tackle one more thing each day. Notice the growth that takes place. Notice the change in your life: your thoughts, emotions, and behaviors and the physical aspects of your health and well-being.

Forgiveness Mantra

Just for today, may I treat myself with kindness, in thought and word, and pardon myself when I realize I may have slipped. Just for today, may I show kindness to another, even if it is not reciprocated. Just for today, may I let go of anger and resentment for myself and others. Just for today, may I let go of sadness and hurt and instead seek happiness and joy.

Just for today, may I acknowledge a triumph or success within myself as well as another. Just for today, may I recognize a lesson that another helped me understand and learn. Just for today, may I recognize a lesson that I allowed myself to understand and learn.

Forgiveness:

One Size Fits No-one

People are often looking for a quick fix or a set of steps that will work for everyone. Forgiveness doesn't work exactly one way; it's a highly individualized process that involves being willing and being ready. That being said, it is imperative for you to be fully engaged with your own heart and then allowing your heart to connect with your brain. Heart and brain coherence are crucial for self-healing. To learn more about this, visit www.hearthmath.org and www.heartmath.com, and check out Dr. Joe Dispenza's vast research on this. I offer a simple breathing technique on my YouTube channel (@The Pursuit Guru) that shows you how to get into a calm state of being—within only three minutes—you can better engage your heart and connect with your brain more freely.

Anything that provides you with feeling nurtured and nourished is a good way to better prepare yourself for deep healing. Here is a little list of just some things you can engage in besides what I've already mentioned: hiking, biking, walking, yoga, sit out in nature, Qi Gong, Tai Chi, meditation, forgiveness mantra, forgiveness processes, journaling or simply writing on paper that of which you want to express, choosing healthier foods, playing relaxing music, playing an instrument, drawing, painting, coloring, gratitude list/journal, find a fun or interesting class or workshop. Pick at least three of the items from the list provided or create a list for yourself and schedule these things into your life as practices. Sometimes "me time" or "healing time" has to be put as an appointment on your calendar—just like going to any sort of doctor or other appointment. This is *your* time and it matters as much as, if not more, than any other appointment you will schedule. Never let anyone take that scheduled time, you let them know you have an appointment—it's none of their business what the appointment is about or whom it's with.

Learn how you want to do forgiveness for yourself and in *your* life. Implement the best practices for *your* utmost well-being.

*One of the most self-centered things you
can do is to be so dysfunctional that you
KNOWINGLY hurt people who love you and
care about you, yet you do not seek the help
that you need. You let others take your pain
for you instead of dealing with it yourself.*

—Jan Aboussafy

Forgiveness:

It Is Yours to Implement

The process of forgiveness I learned is called *Ho'oponopono* and is a traditional Hawaiian process. The Hawaiians use this process on a daily, weekly, and monthly basis, basically whenever the situation calls for it! The idea is to keep *Pono*, which *very loosely* translates as "right with life, right within yourself, balanced, congruent, aligned (mentally, emotionally, physically, spiritually)." I have adapted this process from the teachings of Dr. Matthew James, am using it with permission, and am not attempting to teach it, only share it. I am calling the processes I have recorded the "Forgiveness Process and Self-Forgiveness Process" because I am not teaching about the lineage or history of *Huna*. Very loosely summed up, Huna is a sacred Hawaiian practice using breath, energy, and the elements of our surroundings, such as color, earth, wind, fire, water, and so forth. The Ho'oponopono process is a sacred process and is only to be taught with permission from someone within the lineage.

The Ho'oponopono process is not the only process by which people can forgive, but it is the most powerful and potent process I have come across. I encourage each person to find what works for him or her, and as long as the results are being in a place of forgiveness, keep doing it.

If you choose to use the Ho'oponopono/forgiveness processes, please respect the lineage and origin and only use the recorded processes for you and with yourself.

To download the forgiveness recordings, please visit <u>www.thepursuitofforgiveness.com.</u>

Go forward with forgiveness in your heart and as a practice.

About the Author

Melissa Reese and her husband, Nick, live in Arizona with their three dogs. She loves nature and spends time hiking or simply enjoying the quietude and connection that being in nature provides.

Melissa is a holistic practitioner, teacher, author, and speaker. She has a BA in psychology from Arizona State University and further education from the Southwest Institute of Healing Arts, the Empowerment Partnership, and other training programs. She is a board-certified clinical hypnotherapist, Master practitioner of neuro-linguistic programming (NLP), PSYCH-K practitioner, life coach, and Jikiden Reiki specialist. She has over 1,800 hours of training. Melissa is also the author of The Pursuit of More.

She started her journey in the healing arts as an observer, watching her mom and dad transform their lives in a matter of ten days. Then, she became a client.

Melissa started mainly with hypnotherapy, then NLP, Reiki, acupuncture, and herbs. The work she did profoundly helped her transform her life in a very short period of time. She learned how to clear her anger, how to communicate more efficiently and effectively, and how self-care and self-work are imperative to implement as a regular part of life. Melissa also learned how to be less judgmental and more open and curious regarding what life and people have to offer. She has learned that forgiveness and LOVE are at the crux of any and all healing that can take place. She was so impressed with the improvement and transformation accomplished in such a short time that she decided to pursue this field as a career.

Utilizing the tools and techniques that NLP, Hypnotherapy, Life Coaching, Jikiden Reiki, naturopathic medicine, and other modalities, she has been able to heal herself of auto-immune issues and other chronic illness. She has learned how to have and invite in healthier relationships and establish very important boundaries that support her life and well-being.

Her mission has always been to learn and grow as a person and a practitioner and create positive, permanent change in her life. Her passion is to then utilize that experience, knowledge and wisdom in a practice that encourages and helps to empower others to stand in their power gracefully, creating the best version of themselves.

Melissa helps people break-through and clear their "crap" (mental and emotional baggage) so that they can pursue what has seemed out of reach and experience freedom, joy, happiness, and love more deeply and more often.

She believes we each have the tools to heal ourselves and we must first get out of our own way to be able to access and fully utilize them. She encourages and helps people to CREATE the life they desire to achieve by assisting them in transforming their perceived blocks and barriers and turn them into stepping stones. Within the pursuit lies the journey and within the journey lies the answers.

Melissa loves the path that she is on and her goal is to help people who want to positively change their life, whether it be big or small.

References and Resources:

Books:

Biology of Belief by Bruce Lipton, PhD

The Honeymoon Effect by Bruce Lipton, PhD

Molecules of Emotion by Candace Pert

The True Power of Water by Masaru Emoto

You Can Heal Your Life by Louise Hay

Breaking the Habit of Being Yourself by Dr. Joe Dispenza

Becoming Supernatural by Dr. Joe Dispenza

The Power of TED by David Emerald

Practical Miracles by Arielle Essex

You are a Badass by Jen Sincero

Love, Medicine, & Miracles by Bernie Siegel, MD

The Pursuit of More by Melissa Reese

Presence by Amy Cuddy

The Anatomy of Calling by Lissa Rankin

Mind Over Medicine by Lissa Rankin

Spirit Junkie by Gabrielle Bernstein

The Universe Has Your Back by Gabrielle Bernstein

Finding Your Way In a Wild New World by Martha Beck

Finding Your Own North Star by Martha Beck

The Untethered Soul by Michael A. Singer

Source Field Investigations by David Wilcock

Big Magic: Creative Living Beyond Fear by Elizabeth Gilbert

Screw It, Let's Do It by Sir Richard Branson

The Virgin Way by Sir Richard Branson

Finding My Virginity by Sir Richard Branson

Losing My Virginity by Sir Richard Branson

Videos: (You can find them on Gaia TV and the documentaries' websites.)

What the Bleep Do We Know?

The Cure Is

Choice Point Theory

The Living Matrix

You Can Heal Your Life (Found with Louise Hay's titled book.)

<u>To purchase the forgiveness recordings, and download the free meditation that comes with this book, visit <u>www.thepursuitofforgiveness.com.</u></u>

For blog articles, more information and resources, visit **<u>www.thepursuitguru.com.</u>**

Forgiveness has all the stated reasons and benefits of self-healing and well-being. It can also be thought of as a cleansing tool in which to have a better perspective of the quality of the person you have been led to forgive. Once the prejudices supported by your previously held judgment have been cleared, the other person may take on a more holistic and favorable aspect in your life.
—Kurt Hickenlooper

Want to "forgive it forward?" If you enjoyed this book and know of a family member, friend, co-worker, or organization that would get something from this book, buy a copy for them as a gift. Keep your copy for your continued self-care and healing.

Available on Amazon and Barnes & Noble websites.

CPSIA information can be obtained
at www.ICGtesting.com
Printed in the USA
LVHW031745100220
646431LV00004B/358